A Time to Begin

A Time to Begin

Lewis F. Presnall

First published April, 1987.

ISBN: 0-89486-395-9

Library of Congress Catalog Card Number 87-08234

Printed in the United States of America.

Editor's Note:
   Hazelden Educational Materials offers a variety of information on chemical dependency and related areas. Our
publications do not necessarily represent Hazelden or its
programs, nor do they officially speak for any Twelve Step
organization.

CONTENTS

CHAPTER 1
A TIME TO BEGIN

Have you lost a mate through separation, divorce or death? Have you recently discovered that your child has a serious learning disability? Do you find yourself in need of a mid-stream career change, or has your old career been lost, while a new one has not been selected or found?

When one encounters events like these, what inner and supporting resources does one need? As efforts are made to cope with the problems, how does one exercise and strengthen the spiritual and mental resources? What can you learn from the experiences of zestful survivors which will be helpful to you and others facing these and similar problems?

Everyone has problems, of course, but there are certain kinds of big crises or needs for major change that push us close to our limits.[1] Some of them may not even seem big to other people. It is how a crisis hits you, the impact, not its apparent size, which is the measure of how deeply you feel the hurt. Getting hit by the edge of a board hurts more, and does more damage, than being hit by the flat side.

Usually, the events that shake us to the core are not only big, but close at hand. They leave us asking, "Now what?" Your crisis may have come in the form of treatment for a serious illness or handicapping accident. Or, perhaps you have had a major obligation which bound you to an exclusive task for several years. Finally, it is finished. Re-assessment and re-direction of time, energy, and purpose are now possible and necessary. Someone else may have just completed psychotherapy for an emotional problem, or a period of counseling to overcome the trauma of living with an addicted person.

You may be one of those whose recovery from alcoholism has reached the point where much attention now needs to be given to the Twelfth Step of Alcoholics Anonymous, the one that says, "Having had a spiritual awakening as the result of these steps, we tried to carry this message to alcoholics, and to practice these principles in all our affairs."[2]

Many people need to face a crisis point earlier, several years before they reach the time when it becomes a reality crisis. Such a problem is the planning and preparation for retirement years.

There are other more subtle kinds of problems, which can be devastating, if not met and coped with properly. One of these is the realization that a sense of self-identity has never become well established. Or, a person suddenly becomes aware that there is little true liking for oneself. To paraphrase an old saying, "There is no love lost within oneself!" Since one has never learned to love the self, or to be at home with the self, the ability to love others truly has not been developed either.

Until we have discovered our identity, we also continue to have difficulty in making personal choices that will fit us, and work out for us in time.

Another subtle problem is a major one from which none of us escapes: our own mortality. There is a whole process, concluding with physical death, which one must come to terms with in order to be at home with one's wholeness.

There is a saying among those of us who had to cope with disabilities in our youth or early adulthood. Each one of us expresses the idea in different ways. But the meaning is recognizable: Fortunate are those who recover from a serious disability *early in life,* for they do not go through the remainder of their years with the illusion that they are somehow indestructible, immortal, or omnipotent!

It has been pointed out by many spiritual leaders that we are not fully ready to live until we are fully ready to die. A person can get by on a great deal less than that. But the key word here is "fully." There is a less acute, but more immediate, problem which occurs with some frequency for many of us. There are certain tasks that do not respond to our usual approaches. When we run into one of these, we keep trying different things. We back off and look at the obstacle from other angles. We worry over it, take it to bed at night, and dream about it. There does not seem to be any answer or solution. Yet, this continues to be a problem because it is not one of those things we can walk away from and forget. It seems too important for that.

There are some suggestions we can give here from the experiences of other persons. One of them may be the key to unlocking your puzzle. Whatever the problem or crisis you may have faced, the time to begin dealing with it more constructively is now. No matter how hopeless or depressing your situation may seem, the quality of life does not rest upon some future plan or possibility. The true measure of life's meaning always lies in this moment when one can choose to take either the direction of growth or decay.

A person's life-meaning does not hinge upon how long the human race may last, or whether an individual lives enough years to pursue a career, make a pile of money, or acquire grandchildren. The quality or measure of life's meaning is in whether a person tries today to express love the best way one can. NOW. There is no other ultimate yardstick for human significance. Personal accomplishments, career growth and advancement, or goal achievements are satisfying. But, in and for themselves, they have no ultimate value without the growth of love!

Somehow, the miracle of having a hand in the creative, hopeful process is built into each one of us. We may not have been cooperating very much with it recently. But we do have a choice.

The great personal discoveries are always so simple! When a young couple goes through their first experience of having a baby, they must be awed by the miracle of birth. And also by the fact that they played a part in that. It is an event which mystifies and intrigues the science of biochemistry. This new baby arrives complete with equipment to produce wax for its ears, the know-how to manufacture hundreds of different chemicals in its liver, and a mental computer which presumably will be programmed to manipulate Mama and Papa in six short months. Truly a miracle beyond comprehension. Yet, the parents were part of that creative process. Not merely in the act of conception. They made possible the connection between the creative heritage of preceding generations and, indeed, the whole of humankind.

Another example of the creative life in which we have a hand is our own health. The human body is designed to be healthy, not to be sick. Normally, the body has all kinds of complicated, self-regulating devices for destroying bacteria, immunizing against viral invasion, controlling temperature, providing energy to the body's cells, including the right amount of trace elements, digesting a wide variety of diets, and eliminating waste.

There are many things which we can consciously do to assist these processes — mentally, physically, and emotionally. Modern medicine can also provide us with an enormous variety of increasingly sophisticated health care. But the creative health force is within us. What we and our doctors do is simply to *help* those systems stay functional. So, we can have a hand in our own daily miracle of health.

As you stand at the point of making a new beginning, there are a lot of creative forces ready to respond to your touch. You will also be considering the experiences of the past and your hopes for the future.

Most of the time we look nostalgically upon our past years, as though we were going through a photograph album. When we actually come to the point of making a major decision about life direction, the past must be viewed in a different way. We need to look at past experiences for the lessons they have taught us. Then, we must try to do better with today's decision. If you have been generally successful in life, do not assume that escaping from the domination of that past will be easy. The price for daring to launch into uncharted territory may be very high.

A dramatic example occurred in my office several years ago. A person in no way connected with our organization called and requested a private interview. This was not unusual. The work we did with employee programs within business and industry had received wide publicity. We often had personal requests for interviews from people outside the companies. These came from individuals in public agencies, corporations, and labor unions. The concern could be a personal one or something confidential within their organizations. As time permitted, we always tried to respond.

This appointment was with a man, neatly dressed in a business suit, who appeared to be in his early fifties. He explained that he had decided about a year earlier to make a complete career change. He had resigned from his position in New York City. He and his wife had then spent the next six months selling their house, finishing up their affairs and moving to the campus of a large university, where he had enrolled for the past term, working toward a Master's Degree in industrial psychology.

At the time of our interview, he was between school terms. He had heard about the kind of programs we had in the area of personal employee services and wished to discuss this field with us as part of his own exploration of a future career direction. He was obviously an objective, personable individual, who was accustomed to getting at the core of problems.

The recent experiences at our offices had included an increase in the number of higher-paid persons who had come seeking just this kind of guidance. So, we had a background of suggestions for him.

During our meeting, we established good rapport, so I asked if he would mind telling me how he happened to make such a radical change in his middle years.

He had married shortly after college, and began a steady series of job promotions. He and his wife had apparently continued to be devoted. They had two children, a girl and a boy, both of whom were now young adults and enrolled in colleges. His career moved him into the corporate offices of his company.

He and his wife bought a large house in one of the high-status suburbs of Long Island. They had belonged to a couple of the expensive country clubs and had all of the usual trimmings of that lifestyle.

But, for the prior two or three years, in spite of a career which continued to be very successful, he had become increasingly discontented with his work. It also seemed to him that each member of his family was somehow disconnected from the others. None of them truly talked to the others anymore. He did not feel that his own life had a sense of meaning.

One night, shortly before Christmas, he was working late at his desk. After finishing, he came out of his office, walked past the desks of his secretaries, and looked across the empty floor space of the office tower high above Manhattan. Before him were all the rows of empty desks and office entrances, symbolic in his mind of the people and the bustling activity that occupied the place five days a week.

"All of a sudden," he said, "the question hit me: 'Is this what you want to do the rest of your life?' "

Right away he knew the answer: "No!"

He told the rest of the story quickly. When he discussed his feelings with his wife, she cried a while, mostly with relief that he was taking the time to share with her so openly. Then, they talked and talked — about everything, as they used to do in the earlier years of their marriage. They were supportive of one another and decided to discuss everything with their daughter and son during the Christmas vacation.

After the initial jolt, the response from them was much the same. The sale of the house and reduction of personal property were discussed. College budgets, ways of sharing and supplementing them with earnings were reviewed for ideas. Since the father was also hoping to return to college in the Midwest, that financial need was included in the discussion. The attitude of the two young people was that they were happy to feel Mom and Dad could talk to them like adults. There was confidence that the four of them could somehow work things out, each one carrying a proper share of his or her own load.

The rest is a standard story of a beginning which had its rough spots but was a creative adventure. The big hurdle was to get free from the potential tyranny of what is usually viewed as the rewards of a successful past.

We often overlook another factor about dealing with success. Most of us have had a great deal more experience coping with failure and the deadly average than we have had in dealing with success.

We think we would like the rewards of success but are instinctively afraid of the risks that might be involved. Often when some success does come our way, our inexperience soon enables us to "snatch failure from the jaws of success."

So, our fears of again venturing into the unknown are reinforced!

If that is our background, the uncertainties of the future can be serious obstacles to making a decisive beginning. We have known so little success and so much failure that the reserves of self-confidence are at a low ebb. Much as we would like to make a new beginning, we are more terrified of a new, untried direction than we are of staying put.

In the following chapter we shall make some suggestions about how to deal with fears of this sort and how to gain confidence by starting on small steps toward new beginnings.

Some advisers tell us we should make a start by first building our attitudes of self-confidence. They tell us to think about ourselves in a more positive way. Then we will begin to act more assertively. Well, this works for some people. But attitudes change a lot faster and more permanently if we can begin right away to practice taking a few small steps. As we change action patterns, feelings of accomplishment and attitudes of self-confidence begin to grow.

When you make a commitment to a new direction, you need to put feet to your dreams and your prayers right away. The past is finished. It cannot be changed. The future is not yet available to you. Nothing happens in the future. *Happenings are NOW.*

Although a decision can only be made in the present, you should never see it as an end in itself. For all of us, it is easy to fall into the trap of thinking that if we experience one big emotional insight, a spiritual awakening, or perhaps a burst of maturity through psychotherapy, we will have crossed a threshold where no other big beginning of the same sort will be necessary.

As someone has said, "No growth is possible for those who think they have already arrived." Or, to use the words of another anonymous commentator on the spiritual scene, "No blindness is greater than the eyes of one who, having once touched the hem of divinity's garment, believes he will need no further revelation."

In the usual life span, there are numerous critical decision points, each building upon the previous ones. In between there will be many, many days when the high point experiences are digested and worked into the fabric of daily habit patterns. You should not hold back from making a start because of fears about the future. The best insurance you can have against future risks is the realization that you have just taken the *first* step. Far more is involved in a critical life change than merely sitting down at a table and writing out a set of resolutions, as for the New Year. What you are beginning then is a decision similar to saying, "Today I have decided that, if my sweetheart is agreeable, I am ready to get married." Or, to use a quite different illustration, some people think of a new beginning as saying, "Tomorrow, I resolve to go on the diet my friend used and lose twenty-four pounds."

In contrast, the approach being suggested here is similar to someone saying, "My doctor says I have developed Type II diabetes, and it can probably be handled without insulin, if I change my eating habits. So, today I have *decided to begin* to learn what I should eat and to learn to *enjoy only* those foods and drinks which my body says it needs. Once I learn that knowledge, and acquire those tastes, this will be my lifestyle from then on." (Of course, this is a summary of the mental conversation you might carry on with yourself. In essence, however, you must reach that sort of inner conclusion if the change in lifestyle is to be a comfortable fit with everyday living.)

You will find such an approach to be far more effective — and enjoyable — than a mere set of resolutions to "go on a diet" for a short time.

In both the marriage and the eating habits decision, no one supposes that making the choice is the end of the matter. The initial determination is a first step. Nothing happens until that happens. Afterward, there will be a whole process of change, growth, and long-term actions to follow.

Yet, some of us imagine that commitment to a spiritual way of life is somehow a different process than commitment to marriage, or to a from-now-on eating style. As though it were assumed that if one turned toward God and away from egocentricity, there would thenceforth never be need to reaffirm that commitment.

Such an assumption will not endure close scrutiny. It is flawed in several ways. Just to mention one: It expects a degree of *instant* sainthood from us that is totally beyond us, even with the grace of God. One would have to believe, arrogantly, "Now, I am going to go with God, and I am so certain of myself that I shall never make another misjudgment or misstep as long as I live!"

Ridiculous? Perhaps. Yet, there are some of us whose actions and choices seem to indicate that our spiritual growth had become arrested, or retarded, at the level of an initial awakening several years ago.

We see even more examples of persons who keep repeating the same, tired commitments about intentions to be kinder to their families, cheerful to the neighbors, or diligent about preparing early for holidays. The beginnings are often promising. The follow-through is often disappointing.

What goes wrong in the interim? Perhaps the real difficulty starts at the time when we think a change should be made. We may be too casual about it. But there are deeper problems. We have already mentioned one: the tendency to expect the decision to stand by itself without all of our persistent, daily efforts to make it a zestful, growing, joyful part of our lifestyle.

A classical example (now one which is widely known) is the so-called Tenth Step in the Alcoholics Anonymous program of recovery. In Steps Five, Six, Seven, and Eight the person seeking help through the program has been told that others have found it necessary in recovering from alcoholism to make a beginning of dealing honestly with one's wrongdoing and harm to other people.

Then Step Ten instructs, "Continued to take personal inventory and when we are wrong promptly admitted it."[3] This Step is a recognition that keeping oneself in creative relationship with other people requires continuing effort. The readiness to renew apologies and make amends to others is essential to the spiritual life in keeping it awakened. Nothing blocks the flow of spiritual juices like resentment or guilt feeling toward someone. We have to keep reminding ourselves to apologize *promptly* when we are wrong. A good rule to follow is, "When in doubt about who started the rupture in the relationship, apologize anyhow." Persons familiar with Biblical literature may be reminded of the admonition from the book of Ephesians, ". . . do not let sunset find you still nursing (your anger)."[4] Some of us have learned from our own bodies the deadly internal effects of anger's adrenalin when nursed into resentment. We have painfully discovered that adrenalin, one of the body's servants, can also become a destroyer. It does not make a great deal of difference whether the anger is "justified" by another person's actions or not.

If there is any way to make amends for the wrong without doing further harm or injury, you should do that also.

The mechanism of the internal shot of adrenalin within our bodies is an emergency lifesaving device. It equips humankind for life-threatening situations by preparing the body to right or run away very fast. There are occasions when we still need this mechanism. However, in the modern office, shop, or social scene the responses are seldom useful. If our own immaturities cause us to "shoot up" frequently with this powerful drug, we usually need to do something about getting our emotions reorganized. After that, if we occasionally experience extreme anger at someone, we usually need to defuse it quickly.

Often, when we cool off, we find that we had a hand in creating the situation, and we *need to apologize or make amends.* It would be neat in this age of communicating by bumper stickers if we might see one that says, "HAVE YOU APOLOGIZED TO ANYONE LATELY?" A second hazard to a promising beginning is that of peer pressure. The person who tries to follow a spiritually committed lifestyle also lives in a society where many persons are impelled and motivated quite differently at the core. Their outward behavior may often look similar to that of the committed person, but, inwardly, there are different value systems. For instance, in some circles it is advised, "Never apologize for anything." In many large organizations, the *unwritten rules of survival include:*

1. Never apologize or admit to a mistake. Cover it with jargon.
2. Never take direct responsibility for fixing anything. Hedge and qualify.
3. Never resign a position if one feels a policy is wrong; try for a transfer to another division or department.

In such a social atmosphere, the person who is committed to taking personal responsibility for behavior in public life has to be vigilant about the dangers of alibis and excuses for fudging on the rules of one's spiritual track.

Another example is the constant din of suggestions, appeals to mediocrity, and humorless self-interests, which make it difficult to keep one's focus upon the primary sense of inner direction. The background noises and the multitude of voices one constantly hears are a steady din. The messages range all the way from spiritual confusion to directed egocentricity.

The need for spaces of inner silence is the reason why all spiritual groups and disciplines urge their committed people to set aside some definite period, or periods, each day for meditation, prayer, and/or devotional reading.

You need to renew the conversation with the inner voice of universal consciousness. Or, at the very least, find some time during the day when the clamor of uncommitted voices is not intruding full volume into your mind. If the regular quiet time has been set aside and you open the mind to God's presence, there will sometimes be occasions when nothing elevating seems to enter the thoughts.

That is all right. A period of quietness and relaxation is not without its uses.

More often than not, however, a refreshed clarity of direction, or a sense of deep joy, will emerge. This will color the whole day, if you are meditating in the morning; or add to a restful night, if the quiet time is just before sleep.

Many of us prefer to have short times of meditation both at the beginning and at the end of a day, perhaps in addition to a longer session at some other hour. Schedules depend, in part, upon the hours of one's daily work and family activities.

Some men like to say a short prayer of reaffirmation while they are shaving in the morning; and women when they are applying their makeup. (The bathroom is a great invention for a place of privacy in a hurried world — provided, of course, that someone has not introduced a telephone, radio, or TV set with the misguided notion that even here one should not be left alone with God!)

The conclusion of the day is a good time to sign off with a thought of thanks and benediction.

These beginning-of-the-day invocations, and end-of-the-day benedictions are often phrased in very informal, folksy language.

For example, in describing them to a close friend, a person may say something to this effect, "In the morning, I stand in front of the mirror in the bathroom. There is something unflattering about looking at my reflection in the early morning. So, I may say, 'Well, God, here I am again. It is a new day. With your guidance, I will try to put my best into today.'

"Then, just before bedtime that night, perhaps I may say, 'Thank you, God for being with me today. There were some times when I did not do too well. You and I know what I did wrong. Forgive me, and thank you for being with me and teaching me.' "

People who follow routines similar to this, plus regular occasions for devotional reading or longer periods of meditation, universally report that two results follow. First, the initial commitment, or beginning, is maintained with greater security than if they try to coast along on yesterday's euphoria. Second, there is a generally upward trend in spiritual and personality growth. Certainly, there are dips and valleys in the process. Or perhaps, a better word would be "pauses," while inner growth is consolidated.

Actually, this is the way growth occurs in the physical body during youth, and in the acquisition of new skills in maturity. Remember, in your childhood how there were periods when weight and height were added quite rapidly. At other times, these changes were less evident, but muscles and functions were strengthened and toughened.

When one is in the process of acquiring a new skill, the same sequence occurs. There will be periods of obvious advancement. At other times, days may pass without our being able to discern much change. It is likely that these slow periods will be followed by another spurt in growth.

So, as you experience levels of spiritual awareness, you will often be reminded of the ups and downs in the years of physical development in childhood. Or, there may be comparisons with times when you were taking music lessons, learning a physical sport, or a skilled trade.

Is it not revealing how similar are the processes of growth, whether they be physical, mental, emotional, or spiritual? *Another evidence of the wholeness built into humankind!*

It has become fashionable in recent years to talk about holistic medicine. We sometimes wonder how much real understanding there is of its meaning, or whether the phrase is being used because people merely wish so desperately that more health professional teams would treat us as though we were people.

But another question should perhaps be asked. It may be more at the heart of the matter: How many of us perceive ourselves whole? Physically, mentally, emotionally, and spiritually? Altogether as a single set of functions?

Just having the capacity to so perceive one's person is an enormous step toward a higher level of spiritual, emotional, mental, and physical existence. We are not speaking here about miracles or levels of attainment which are seldom achieved.

You can begin to move in that direction. The avenues of creativeness have been well scouted, well explored, and thoroughly mapped. You can learn to do what others have done. You can move along at your own speed toward an increasing sense of wholeness.

Let us move along, then, into some of the reliable avenues of creative beginnings.

CHAPTER 2
TAKE CHARGE OF YOUR LIFE

For most of us, the first opportunity to take full charge of our personal lives is when we leave the financial support of our parents and establish our own residence address. It is usually a time of anticipation and excitement. Part of the excitement is the anxiety about how we will approach full responsibility for the decisions of independent living. Some of these will be personal budgeting, scheduling of work and recreation hours, and being the complete decision-maker about social relationships, house guests, house furnishings tastes, or lifestyles. If one has teamed up with a roommate or roommates, arrangements will be needed for agreement and scheduling of household duties.

At first, the privileges of being one's own boss may be so exhilarating that excessive debts or social obligations can undercut our newly found independence. During young adult years, most of us have some difficulties of this sort. When one's income is low in proportion to financial need — or wants — a minor choice made too hastily can deprive one of a major objective.

The Influence of Other People

This phrase is preferable to the currently popular terms of *peers* or *significant others*. The first limits influences to those in one's immediate group or age level; whereas, the influences we wish to consider here include a wider range of people. Many of them may be older relatives or acquaintances, in-laws, or even individuals we perceive as role models, even though we do not know them personally.

The latter term, *significant others,* smacks too much of the jargon borrowed from the field of psychology. (There is nothing wrong with technical jargon in its proper place, but it means little to individuals outside a specialized field.) For our purposes, the term simply lacks the common depth of meaning of the phrase, *the influence of other people.*

In our childhood we are shaped and educated by the opinions, examples, and teachings of other people. Our own brothers and sisters, if we have them, are included. To the degree that we remain flexible and curious, other people continue to shape and educate us during adult years also.

I have a swimming partner. We meet regularly every weekday morning before breakfast for a half hour in the pool. On the mornings when we both arrive with exuberance and share a bit of laughter, it gives us an extra lift for the day. If one of us has had a restless night's sleep and arrives a little grumpy, we still enjoy our exercise, but the mood is less exhilarating.

To carry this illustration a bit further, each one of us has worked at several things and acquired some expertise in certain fields. If we encounter a situation where another's knowledge would be helpful, we ask for comment.

After seeking advice, we

1) make up our own minds,
2) take whatever action is appropriate, and
3) expect, of course, to assume full responsibility for the choice.

The one who gave the advice

1) takes care not to intrude upon the privacy of the other's decision, and
2) is in no way affronted if the other person finds the advice unsuitable.

Without ever discussing these matters, those relations are natural and comfortable, since both of us have long since acquired the habits of being in charge of our personal lives.

But, neither of us got to that state of affairs overnight. *We had to learn how to do it by ourselves,* just as everyone does!

If you find that your personal decisions are too greatly dominated by the opinions and influences of others, you have solved perhaps 70 percent of the problem when you can identify the specific changes which you need to make. It will help if you ask yourself, "In what way am I too tied to the opinions of others?" and "Why have I felt this need to remain dependent, or compliant?" Is it fear of failure? Is it fear of disapproval? Is it fear of losing someone, or something, of value? Or, is it now merely an old habit?

If you can identify the strings that hold you, you can better decide how and when to sever those ties. You need to know what the risks are, and be willing to assume them, before you choose another course of your own.

Once you make a decision, be prepared *cheerfully* for the worst and hope for the best. If the thing is *truly* right for you, it will be right for you.

The Domination of Circumstances

Some persons form the habit of surrendering to circumstances their right of choice.

A close friend's older sister had gotten into the habit of postponing both large and small decisions with the excuse, "I'll wait and see what happens; something always comes up." On important matters, what increasingly "came up" was that someone else — a relative or her accountant — had to step in and provide her with specific alternatives. Over time, there were two side effects. First, she progressively lost the will and know-how of independence. Second, many minor decisions were neglected, because associates and relatives had neither the time nor the wish to play parent for her.

Other examples come to mind from the world of business and industry. Within sizable organizations we often observe conditions where many key people become discontented with the policies or administration. After a time, if the problems are not resolved, perhaps two or three managers will find positions elsewhere and resign. Some of the others will privately confide that they would also like to leave. But they will not look for other jobs. They stay on, willing to tolerate the frustration, rather than give up the comfort of fringe benefits and accumulated service.

They have become more directed by circumstances than by their own realistic assessment of what might be fulfilling.

The issues here are to be sure we take charge of those areas we can and that we remain alert to avoid the domination of our lives by the circumstances that surround us.

We may not immediately be able to change everything we should. But we can certainly control how we feel about our surroundings, and we can work at making needed changes.

If a person is to be truly in charge of his life, it is absolutely necessary that one exercise both freedom and responsibility at the emotionally adult level. As we become more proficient in being responsibly in charge of our lives, it is noticeable that we continue to grow into a larger humanness.

Balance Between Acceptance and Alteration

The now nearly classic play, *Fiddler on the Roof,* opens with the symbol and the song of the fiddler playing, while precariously standing at the peak of a rooftop. The question is immediately asked as to how the people of this remote village maintain their equilibrium in the midst of their world. The answer is cultural tradition, which specifies everyone's role and the modes of behavior.

The play is really a modern parable which describes the problems of people when the old guidelines and traditions no longer give automatic answers to every question. Apart from its haunting music, this is why the drama has so caught our imagination in a rapidly altered society during this past score of years.

So, how can we find the proper balance today between the things we must accept and the things we should change?

In the words now popularly known as "The Serenity Prayer," Reinhold Niebuhr neatly avoided that issue by simply asking "God grant us — the wisdom to know the difference." But practical man that he was, in addition to being an outstanding theological thinker, he constantly affirmed we had the obligation of faith to live in the world as we found it. We must take the responsibility to care for society, to be involved with trying to live justly and honestly. There would be times when we made choices in these efforts which were later found inappropriate. That is part of the human condition. But we are not all-wise.

Like the wording of his prayer, his theology was full of paradoxes. Yet, paradox is the nature of the spiritual search. So, where do we start in trying to accept the things we cannot change and having the courage to change the things we can?

The only set of guidelines or suggestions upon which all committed "searchers" seem to agree includes the following essentials:

The Pattern of Design That Moves in Human Affairs

First, in whatever way they may come to it or describe it, these people have made a commitment to turn themselves over to the control of God, or a Higher Power, as they understand such a Power. They have either been raised into that way of life since childhood or, more commonly, have encountered experiences that have convinced them an egocentric focus leads to a chaotic, unmanageable existence.

Through those experiences they have found a capacity for the acceptance of
1. things they should not attempt to change.
2. things that might need changing later.

Second, in giving control to a Higher Power, they also express a faith that there is some kind of a process at work, beyond their comprehension, but nevertheless dependable — a benevolent force which will "lead" them, if they trust it.

To many people, that does not make sense, does it?

Well, it apparently strikes the new searcher in much the same way. But such a person has usually made enough of a mess of things through the old egocentric focus that the new alternative has appeal. Guided, usually, by a mentor of more experience, the person sets out on the new course. The trust-filled method quickly demonstrates its workable nature.

Sensing the Design Directions

Contrary to a lot of religious and mystical nonsense about visions, voices, and miraculous inspirations, the searchers here described use very simple, daily yardsticks which are an integral part of their earthy orientation.

First, they try to keep in touch with the person they truly are, giving some attention daily to being internally honest and watching that signs of egocentric control do not creep back in. They try to see themselves in perspective, with a sense of humor, not taking themselves too seriously. Yet, they give themselves to life, to others, to enjoyable tasks at hand.

In other words, they try to keep their inner balance wheels working and well oiled, so they will not lose track of who they are in relation to others.

In taking charge of their options and decisions, they know that the basic tool for this task is the decision-maker: themselves. Having an intimate grasp of what fits them at a given time is of the utmost importance.

The second thing these people try to do can best be described by using some analogies.

Suppose, then, that you have a good general idea about the career, project, or direction you should try to explore. Imagine that this direction is like a long building corridor with many closed doors leading from it on both sides. You start walking along the corridor. As you come to each door, you try the knob of one after another, until you find one unlocked to you.

You think that perhaps this may be the one you should enter. You push it open and look inside. If the place appears to suit your needs, you go in and start to develop the objectives you had in mind from the resources you find there.

If the room is not designed to fit your project or equipped for it, you go along the corridor to other rooms.

Sometimes a door may be unlocked, but things are piled high against the other side. You cannot push it open without applying great or undue force. That is not your opening.

If a door is locked or resists opening, you do not stand there pounding on it or screaming that people or the universe is against you. *These are circumstances you must accept.* You go along to the next door. You may come back at a later time and find the obstructions gone. In that case, you know on the previous occasion it was not the wrong door, but simply the wrong *time* for you.

The doors that open easily (the opportunities that you identify through gentle, objective exploration) are the "leadings" that inform you about the design pattern you should try to follow. They indicate the areas where you can make changes. Within that framework of design, one should direct the best concentrated effort. (Assuming egocentricity and dishonesty have not resumed their dominance of you.)

The remarkable thing about applying those methods is the satisfying results which begin to emerge. Even in a fairly short time, people are always amazed to find what good life structures are emerging and how easily things drop into place.

Over and over, one hears a comment, such as: "Is this all there is to it? And all these years I've been knocking myself out and not getting much done."

You see, one is not trying to produce success anymore. One is merely attempting to function in harmony with oneself and the flow of the universe. How one defines or describes that flow is not particularly important. One simply tries to *keep in tune with what one can and cannot change.*

You have been scanning an overview of the basic approaches to taking charge of your life, as well as major obstacles and some guidelines that can give clues to direction.

Blueprints, design, and superstructure are important parts of any structure. However, nuts and bolts, foundations, and supports are also essential. We need to turn our attention now to these.

What does one need in order to build permanence and dependability? How can one start small and move toward larger actions? If a person has been following a semi-organized lifestyle for years, what daily exercises will help to strengthen one's sense of order and control?

Using Time as an Asset

The summer of 1930 was a time of transition in the United States, indeed, throughout the entire industrialized world. The October 1929 New York Stock Market crash was only a few months past. The full effects of what would later be called the Great Depression were not yet upon us, but jobs were beginning to get scarce, especially for unskilled, young adults.

24

It is also personally recalled as a time of transition. I had just graduated from high school and was considering whether, where, and how to finance a possible enrollment in college. A combination of illnesses and slowed economy had already wiped out the possibility of more than token family support for college expenses. The options lay between working my own way through, or finding some kind of steady job and not going to college.

There is no particular recollection of pressure. Physical vigor and youth were too vibrant for that. Still, the daily background awareness was attentive to the completion of adulthood skills of my own. A temporary summer job as clerk in the only men's wear store of our small town provided a wage of seventeen dollars per week. (Board and room could be had at that time in many towns for $15 a month.) The hours were long — seven to five Monday to Friday, and seven to eight on Saturdays — shared with the owner. So there were many occasions when no customers needed attention, and I could think about more creative options than keeping merchandise in order and collecting wages at the week's end.

In that atmosphere, an older friend dropped by the store one day and presented me with a completely unexpected gift. It was a book, a copy of *How to Live* by the British novelist, Arnold Bennett. One of the very first self-help, self-improvement books, this 1925 United States edition from the Garden City Publishing Co. in New York was a collection of four earlier booklets copyrighted by an English publisher, George H. Doran Co: "How to Live on Twenty-Four Hours a Day" (1910), "The Human Machine" (1910), "Mental Efficiency and Other Hints to Men and Women" (1911), and "Self and Self-Management" (1918).

As a demonstration that there is hardly anything new under the sun, most of the ideas in this volume are as apt and modern as if they were penned seventy years later. The most noticeable difference is that the writing is more polished and precise than the staccato style which seems necessary today in retaining attention.

The first section, covering only 75 pages, made such an impression upon me that I studied it thoroughly and have retained the book in my personal library to the present day. More than any one thing, other than the skilled trades which my building contractor father tried to reach me, Bennett's suggestions enabled me, subsequently, to work my way through college.

Bennett calls attention to the daily miracle of time. A person wakes up in the morning and finds available a new supply of 24 hours — "the unmanufactured tissue of the universe of your life." This is all yours. Whether you are rich or poor in money or social station in life, there is no difference. Everyone gets the same amount of time each day. Neither does it matter whether you have used your time wisely, or squandered it, the previous day.

Also, no one can steal this asset from you.

Neither can you draw an advance on the future allowance. You cannot get into debt. You can only waste the passing moment. You cannot waste tomorrow! You cannot even waste the next hour. It is kept for your arrival at that hour.

People can pile up money and property in incredible heaps. The "supply of time, though gloriously regular, is cruelly restricted." You cannot alter anything by saying, "I wish I had more time." The only alteration possible is improved management of the daily allotment you receive.

We may have little control over the space we occupy. We have nearly total control over the way we manage our time within that space. Whether it rains or shines, whether we are well-thought-of or despised, our time remains our greatest asset. How we develop it, how we use it, is our choice.

Skill in the management of time is not acquired by reading about it. The reading only draws upon the experience of others to give us step-by-step instructions for different situations.

For instance, it was not until fourteen months after reading Bennett's material that I put his more detailed suggestions into full practice — by necessity. The occasion was enrollment at a college 800 miles from home. For the start, I had a one-year loan of just enough money to cover two semesters' tuition. The amount was approximately what could be saved by working and living in the hometown the following summer.

A sharp-pencil estimate showed that an average of four hours' work a day, including Saturdays, would be necessary during the school year to cover fees, books, room, board, clothes, and miscellaneous expenses. Presumably, the tuition loan could be rolled over for another school year the next fall.

Immediately after registration, the class hours were entered each week for the semester on calendar squares large enough for write-in of schedule details. As study assignments became clearer during the first two weeks, minor adjustments were made in the time management.

Main categories of my time provided regularly for classes, study time for each, work hours each day, time allotted for meals, sleeping, dressing, grooming, doing laundry and mending clothes, recreation, worship, and school activities. The latter were very limited that first year. Also, there appeared to be no slack for the cost of a trip home at Christmastime.

It was a rigorous, but very educational, experience for a young fellow of eighteen years. However, Bennett's advice had stressed the need for flexibility in allowing time for relaxation. So, I had been careful to include spaces in the schedule for physical exercise and fun things.

It was a revelation to discover just how healthy one could remain when totally focused upon an objective where one was *in charge* of the daily use of time.

During the last third of the second semester, around the end of April and the first of May, there was a new and odd sensation of mental fatigue that kept occurring often in the middle of the week. It was puzzling. Efficiency did not seem to be impaired. The feeling never became that acute. At the time, I thought it was caused by going through the same general routine for so long.

Through experiences in later years, I discovered that the feeling was a symptom of the peculiar fatigue related to chronic overstimulation. Today's term would probably be "burn-out," which is also used as a name for feelings having other multiple causes. In a later chapter on "The Care and Maintenance of the Brain," we will talk about remedies for this sort of fatigue.

A rigorous schedule, such as that just described, may not fit your need at all. If your life has been dominated by the calendar and the clock, using time as an asset could mean that you need to escape from the measurements of time to a more flexible project-oriented time investment.

A friend, who had retired from public school teaching, told us with amusement, "You know, I had been retired for about a year before it suddenly occurred to me that I didn't *have* to do my laundry on Saturdays."

It was at this point she truly began to resume charge of her use of time in many other areas of her life. She was pleased to discover how her days became freed to begin activities that had previously been closed because of the Monday through Friday work schedule, plus lesson plans, during the school year.

She had the asset of her pensions for support, but her big resource, time, had not truly been available for her full use. It had still been dominated by the old, mental habit of a clock and a calendar imposed by others.

The needs of individuals are very different when it comes to taking charge of each day's gift of 24 hours. Mine are today much different from those of a freshman earning his way through college. Your needs will also be the individual product of past experiences, and what seems to fit your identity, as you perceive these factors today.

Start Where You Are and Start Small

When you stop to consider the matter, you realize that taking charge of your life always starts easiest when close to home base and when undertaken in small, measurable bites. After the momentum gets under way and effects begin to multiply in geometric proportions, you may be led far afield and into a dramatic unfolding of unexpected scope.

If you are a younger person, it may surprise you to know that these needs — to start where you are and start small — are as important for an older, richly experienced individual as they are for a younger person.

For example, with permission from members of the family, we share the following excerpt from a tender expression of love and perception. It is from a letter of Catherine McKibben Kim in South Korea to her brother and sisters on the occasion of the death of their father, Frank M. McKibben, February 16, 1984, at age 95:

The mists of time have enveloped another spirit, concealing it from our view and leaving us with only footprints. In fact, Dad has been veiled in mists for some time now, and his footprints have been fewer and lighter. But it is hard to realize that memories are all that remain.

I rather envy Dad. He has moved on to another dimension and is in the process of finding answers to the questions he was asking on his "pilgrimage," perhaps finding answers to questions he did not even think to ask.

We are left to deal with our sense of loss — a missing piece in a long family relationship, with the sense that time marches on and we too are mortal. However, as with any other situation, mental attitude is the key. We can move from the pain of loss to the appreciation of the beauty which is always there to be discovered in life. When I talked to Mom she had *already begun with small things;* lovely flowers, a skating performance, the wonderful solace of friends. Nothing dramatic — *you just start where you are.*

(Italics ours.)

Whether you have been previously dominated by others, circumstances, and/or your own immature urges; or whether you are in need of rearranging your life, the issues are quite basic. Your efforts will primarily be made in the direction of your personal habits and choices.

Fortunately, at this point you are not trying to solve the problems of the world or even attempting to reconstruct your neighborhood.

If you are beginning to set your own adult course, in contrast to the other forces that had previously controlled it, the first small steps are

1. deciding what things you must say no to.
2. deciding how best to say that.

Most people defeat their purpose here. They try to find an alibi or a logical excuse to give for their "no." That is usually a mistake. No matter how reasonable one may sound, others can find equally persuasive reasons why you should continue to respond with a "yes."

The very best turnoff is to say, "I do not choose to do that anymore." But this is often too threatening for the beginner, especially if the "no" is being used to assert one's will against someone whose wishes you had previously followed.

It is a positive inner reinforcement, and outer assurance, if the refused action or direction can immediately be replaced with an affirmative action. For instance, suppose you have become something of a slave to constant complaints about health ailments on the part of a relative or friend. You have found that this does no good for the complaining person, while it consumes great amounts of your time.

You have decided, for the sake of your own time and peace of mind, not to listen to these endless, repetitive monologues any more. You might phrase the refusal in a statement, such as, "I am not going to listen to that anymore. However, if you are not satisfied with the diagnoses of your physician, why don't you ask for a referral to another for examination and a second opinion?"

One of the important elements about staying in charge of one's life is the art of saying no very gently, but very firmly. Like any art, you will get better at it as you practice doing it. At first, there will be times when you fumble the situation, usually because of either lack of firmness, a tendency to explain too much, or leaning in the other direction of being unnecessarily brusque.

Remember, there will always be people who are only too happy to advise you, influence you, sell you something, or get your help with *their* projects. They are not prepared to live your life for you in the sense of bearing your risks, taking responsibility for your future, or assuming the consequences, if the decisions they urged you to make turn sour!

You can accept advice. You should often seek it for the benefit to be had from those with experience and knowledge. But you are the only person who can, and should, assume responsibility for your own decisions. So, do not be apologetic for making them. If your decisions later prove to be in error, you can use them for making fewer future mistakes.

The initial taking charge period may be longer or shorter, depending upon how extensive are the alterations you need to make. For instance, if you have lost a greatly loved mate, and prior to that loss the two of you each had well-established independent interests, the adjustment period will take some time. However, the *initial* time needed to consider your own individual identity and decide upon future activities may not take long. On a scale of one to ten, the time required might be one.

At the other end of the range, if you have recently recovered from a long, seventeen-year, progressive history of prescription-drug dependency and the processes of self-identity had become muddled during those years, your needs will be different. On the time scale, the initial steps might rank between seven to ten. You will experience marked improvement along the way, but it will take time to think through all the areas of your self-identity. Getting to the point where the actions suitable to your new life-choices are habitual will take even longer.

After all, it took a long time for drugs to become so dominant in your life. Be patient with yourself about taking some time to complete the recovery. This is a point where you should be gentle with yourself. Remember, you are not unlimited in capacity just because you are drug-free!

These kinds of problems are *not unique* to recovery from alcohol and other drug dependency. After all, following my own experience of getting ambulatory after polio and then going back to work full time, it took *three more years* of special, daily exercise just to shift from the use of two crutches to the regular use of two canes.

So, stay on your central course. Be content to grow a little each day. If the improvement is the sort of thing which is very slow, do not measure it too often. Do a self-comparison every two weeks, or every six months — whatever is appropriate.

If you become uncertain about your course in a world of many conflicting voices and needs, or if you are a little confused, look again at your central beginnings.

When in Doubt, Recheck Your Identity

Who are you? What processes brought you to a sense of self-identity? Has some egocentricity crept back into the picture? How about your commitment to a Higher Power? Has there been some reversion to grandiosity or to inappropriate dependency?

If everything seems solid at the center, have you begun to listen to the voices that ask you to help solve *all* the problems of a troubled world? You cannot do that, you know, not if you are truly serious about investing the quarter of a century of your time that would be needed to make even a thimble-size dent upon many of these big issues.

In that connection, young adults sometimes inquire with a tone of skepticism, "Can one person have any effect at all upon world affairs, or even upon the country?"

Of course, in part, the question reflects the generally poor or shallow knowledge of so many people about past or recent history. It may also reflect today's emphasis upon quick results. The question, however, is a serious one and deserves a forthright attempt to answer.

Taking full charge of one's life is a much more hopeful process, if at least the *possibility* can be seen that the effort may make some difference to the advancement of humankind.

No person is in a position, ever, to assess truly his or her contribution to humankind. However, all over society's current landscape are strewn the evidences of individuals who

1. knew what they could do,
2. decided what direction would be fun to do it in, and
3. continued to work at that thing long enough to make their dents upon society highly visible.

Of course, one person can make a difference! But you do not start out primarily for that purpose. You get focused because the focus fits you. You extend that because it is fun to do the things well which fit you well. You do not know what the results will be in their broader influence when you start. But if you stay focused, the miracles of creativity begin to occur.

CHAPTER 3
LIVING ONE NOW AT A TIME

The art of mental concentration upon the present has many uses. Escape artists, such as Houdini, knew that survival and success depended as much upon the ability to concentrate totally as upon technical skills. He spent many hours practicing his powers of mental focus.

As examples, watch the intensity of concentration mirrored in the faces of great musicians during major performances. On TV broadcasts, you may have observed the pause and gathering of thought as a weight lifter poises for an extreme effort; or the seconds taken for mental visualizing by an Olympic ski jumper prior to starting down the slope.

If you should go to a Grand Master chess exhibition, watch the visiting champion's concentration while playing twenty or thirty simultaneous games against a group of local experts.

Movie stunt men learn to survive the most difficult feats by concentrating upon the moment of performance. The best of them have been known to admit that achieving 100 percent concentration for a span of four to five minutes is about the maximum time they have been able to achieve, even after years of practice.

For centuries, the value of mental focus upon the present has been recognized among many philosophical groups and world religions. Ancient religious books speak about the discipline of going alone into some solitary place for a period of meditation and disciplined prayer.

The literature of mysticism in various religions is full of references to the levels of spiritual attainment and mental concentration. Long before recent parapsychological research, ancient mystics had discovered methods for successful performance of various feats, which often defy the usual forms of scientific investigation. There is so much we do not yet know about consciousness and the human mind. This is probably one of the great unexplored frontiers.

Another example of the age-old concern with the present moment is the need people often feel not to *overload* their mental circuits with regrets about the past, or anxiety about the future. For instance, there is Jesus' expression found in St. Matthew's Gospel, "Each day has troubles enough of its own." Often, we do well to cope with the problems that need today's attention.

Agony over the past and anxiety about the future are excess baggage. We do not need these extra burdens.

All the above examples, however, are concerned with times of unusual need — periods of excessive preoccupation with past and future, or persons who are striving for extraordinary levels of performance.

It is only in the twentieth century, and especially since the 1930s, that a new emphasis has developed among an increasing number of people. Many more of us have been discovering the gratification, and the need, to focus upon living one day at a time. We can also use the approach of living one NOW at a time.

Living One NOW at a Time

This century, more than any previous time in a changing world history, has been a period of explosively rapid global alterations. The good news is that we live in an era of great opportunities. The bad news is the stress of adaptation we constantly face.

Learning to focus upon the NOW possibilities is not a route of escape from awareness that this is a complex, interrelated world. It is emotionally adult to recognize the reality that one is a part of the whole human family. In contrast, we are moving toward emotional sickness when we become fretful and worried about fixing all of the out-of-kilter things about the universe and its contents.

Even in pursuit of deep religious concerns one's dedication can contribute to emotional collapse. Thomas R. Kelly (1893-1941), a Quaker mystic whose most popular book, *A Testament of Devotion,* was widely read a few decades ago, became obsessed with a twin-striving for spiritual perfection and academic status.[1] Subsequently, a surrender of egocentricity led him into the fulfillment of an integrated person. However, the effects of the prior years of inner conflict undoubtedly left their imprint upon the tissues. They probably contributed to his sudden and untimely death at only 48.

One cannot help making a comparison with another devout Quaker, one of Kelly's mentors, Rufus Jones, who balanced his personal equation of the inner spiritual search with his founding of the American Friends Service Committee. Aside from the social good accomplished, Jones always seemed to be fervent in seeking without being feverish in striving. He survived productively to age eighty-five.

The people who seem to be dealing most effectively and constructively with the vast changes of our times are those who are centered upon two efforts:

1. They exert the choice to reduce the dominance of egocentricity by committing themselves to a Higher Power, as they understand such a Power.
2. They focus upon handling each day as responsibly and as joyfully as they can.

At the beginning you will probably start by trying to focus your attention upon living one day at a time. That is where most of us started. We got out of bed in the morning, and we began with the thought that this is a brand-new day we had been given.

Yesterday is past. We may have done well with some of it. At other points, not so well. But yesterday is past. Today is a new one. Untarnished. Untested. Unknown. Waiting for us to arrive at each moment.

"Today, I shall try to focus upon today — attempting to do the best in each encounter, each task, each moment, that I can. Trying to savor and enjoy the freshness and beauty of each moment. Trying to be as sensitive to other persons as I can. Trying to live this day as though it were the only one I had."

This is the way one might think to himself in the morning. For, indeed, it *is* the only day that one has! We tried to do something like this in the beginning. And so persistent individuals have tried to continue each day since, through all the many intervening years.

Yet, we soon discovered that there were occasions when it was necessary instead to live each ten minutes at a time, or even one minute at a time, rather than the larger time frame of one day.

There were occasions when great pain, or stress, or risk placed us in a pressure cooker of circumstances. We could only cling to the shreds of our composure by concentrating upon getting through one short time span after another. Even one day, or possibly one hour, at a time would be beyond our strength.

These were emergency measures used to get us through severe crisis points. For the most part, however, we gradually settled into a routine of increasing proficiency in the art of living with the primary focus upon one day at a time.

And, then, over a period of years a strange kind of new awareness began to develop for some of us. Increasingly, we found ourself shifting into consciousness of living a now-at-a-time. We shall consider various effects of this in later chapters, but for the moment we shall try to describe how the subtle, yet markedly different awareness evidenced itself in personal feelings and experiences.

Experiencing a New Awareness

One of the first persistent shifts in one's awareness is similar to the fresh view of life experienced by people who thought they had a fatal illness or accident and then were given a reprieve from death.

If you have had such an experience, you will recall the feelings. Perhaps you had an experience in a critical care unit of a hospital where you knew death was close. Or, you might have waited for the results of laboratory tests of the type that, if positive, would identify a fatal, incurable ailment, but, if negative, clearly indicated a treatable condition and normal health ahead. Whatever the circumstances, you will no doubt remember vividly the feeling of rebirth when the crisis had passed. You found yourself appreciating the sparkling, new day of your shiny new beginning.

A similar feeling came with one's initial spiritual awakening.

There was a sense of wonder at the beauty of simple things. You were amazed at how good it was to be alive. You may have thought that never again would you take dew on the grass or the singing of birds for granted.

Possibly, you resolved to be kinder in the words you said to people, or at least you would try to be more sensitive to those around you. Some of the things that you considered important just a few weeks before, now seemed rather trivial. You may have decided to place a different scale of values upon your choices.

This kind of awareness and these kinds of feelings are similar to those which some of us gradually awoke to after a few years of living more or less steadily in a now-at-a-time focus.

But there was one important difference. Usually, the fresh, new-day feeling of the person who gets a reprieve from death or who has an emotional, spiritual awakening tends to fade after a time. One is never quite the same after the experience; however, a person tends to get busy and drop back into the former patterns of thinking.

With the person accustomed to living in the present the exercise *becomes a continuing pattern.* Living in the moment increasingly becomes an awareness which runs along close below the surface of whatever thoughts and activities are receiving practical attention.

The inner excitement of being in touch with a vital, present reality is seldom far from consciousness. There is no stimulant, no outer event or thing, which can produce a feeling comparable to this quiet elation of being at home in the NOW.

There is another noticeable shift in a person's awareness. It is usually first observed after a few years when one thoughtfully encounters the event of death. The most common situation where the change in attitudes may be noted in oneself is when a close relative dies. There are opportunities to hear the comments of other surviving relatives or friends.

Usually they will make a great effort to speak with kindness and to share words of comfort. If they and the deceased person belongs to a religious group, there will be efforts to memorialize the memories by reference to life hereafter that suits the beliefs of the religious group.

Suddenly, the person who has been practicing living in the focus of the present will discover two things:

1. There is no felt need to affirm hope or meaning by asserting that the departed person has moved into some life hereafter.
2. The eternity all these people are referring to as "out there or somehow quite difference from here" is not *here* or *there* or *tomorrow,* but instead is *now,* and was now in every moment that the deceased person experienced, or may presently, be experiencing consciousness.

It may even come somewhat as a shock for one to discover that a shift seems to have taken place. Somehow, one has apparently moved into a different area of self-consciousness, or awareness, from that which was known a few years before. One may wonder whether he or she is feeling something rare or unusual. Or, perhaps it only appears so because many persons have had such experiences and been reluctant to speak about something that does not seem to be widely understood.

The Split Second of the Present

Certainly the concept of the Eternal Now in religious mysticism is not a new idea. It has not received as much favorable attention in recent years.

That is not surprising. Some of the writers who were most enthusiastic about the idea of the Eternal Now made a serious mistake. During the first half of this century they were riding the popular crest of a fad. Like many people enjoying sudden popularity, their writings became a bit grandiose. Taking some reports of deeply spiritual seekers, they tried to stretch these experiences into a philosophical tent large enough to cover many obscure mysteries of the universe.

We do not know why people insist upon making that error again and again. In spite of historic lessons, when some of us stumble onto something new, based upon genuine experience, we cannot seem to resist trying to base a whole structure of card houses upon it.

Nevertheless, if the peace of mind needed to cope effectively with the realities of death, life, disaster — and even success — is found so persistently through living in the present, something real must be occurring.

So, let us look more closely at the notion that in this mortal existence on planet Earth the point where we experience eternity is in the split second of present consciousness.

41

The concept begins with the assumption that we are *more likely* to know reality in the present point of action and awareness than we are to find it in either memory or imaginative projection. The past and the future lend themselves very easily to a world of fantasy.

One can build a good argument for the notions that no creative thing gets done without imagination, and that fantasy plays an important part in that process. We shall consider some of those thoughts shortly. At the moment, however, it should be stressed that the word *realization* comes from the word *real*. The point of realization is the present.

So, the assumption *is* that this present split second, or this moment of awareness, is the point of knowing, experiencing, and consciously touching reality — the reality of whatever it means to say "oneself," and whatever is meant by ultimate reality.

There is no other true awareness point.

The concept is in no sense an explanation. Doubtless, if we accept it, we are not more knowledgeable thereby. Only in the sense of wisdom referring to a grasp of wholeness, does the concept add to our wisdom.

To focus primarily upon the present is simply a method of spiritual living.

Through experience, humankind has learned better methods for promoting physical and mental health. But these methods do not necessarily add much to our knowledge about genes, chromosomes, or body chemistry.

Just so, living in the present does not provide a person with an intimate knowledge of either the nature of God, nor the functions of subatomic particles.

The method does give access to continuing spiritual growth, new levels of awareness, a capacity to cope in fulfilling ways with the issues of human mortality, and an inner reservoir of zest.

How does this focus affect
1. future planning,
2. the world of "what-if's,"
3. yesterday's regrets, and
4. one's assumptions about a Power greater than oneself?

Future Planning

The first reaction of many people is to ask, "You mean one should live without trying to plan for the future?"

Do not confuse living one day *at a* time with living *only for* today.

Instead, our intent is to focus upon living most fully in the present — fully aware, free of anesthesia, totally conscious — aiming at the point of being reasonably true to ourselves.

That also means a person will be using many present moments to plan for the future. Designing the use of future days, weeks, and months of the calendar will be a significant part of *one's present thoughts.*

In fact, as you develop the habit of living in the present, you will become much more skillful in planning your life. You will find there is greater freedom from anxiety in your choices. You will be able to project options on squares of the calendar. It will not be necessary to act out so many choices in view of other people. Instead, you may become adept at projecting your various ideas on paper in the privacy of your home.

It is much easier to make preliminary trial runs on paper and change them with an eraser, or by redoing your schedule, than it is to verbalize them to friends and neighbors. Then, when an option is discarded, you do not need to explain why you changed your mind again!

The World of WHAT-IF's

The world of what-ifs is the world of our dreams and fantasies. It is also the mental-emotional area of our anxieties and fears.

These are the processes of imagination and invention — one of the higher powers of consciousness — which distinguishes humankind from the nonhuman. In imagination we have the potential for both the very best behavior and the very worst behavior people have exhibited throughout the history of humankind.

Some people are afraid of fantasy. When they think their children are daydreaming or becoming too interested in the arts of poetry or painting, they try to discourage these interests. If young people in such families wish to choose careers in artistic fields, the parents may argue that the option is impractical. This occurs most frequently in homes where few, if any relatives, have shown artistic aptitudes.

The circumstances can lead to sad and frustrating experiences.

Quite apart from career decisions, fantasy has two very practical uses: It puts the mind into free flight where the intuitive parts of our brain-computers can work. Fantasy cuts across the slower, logical connectors and provides clues to creative answers.

If no logical answer to a complex problem seems possible, intuition is an alternative. Some persons use the technique of simply getting into a relaxed mental state just before bedtime. Then, they focus upon the problem objectively and without anxiety for a few minutes. Usually, after they awake the next day, a new clue to a feasible solution would emerge in the conscious mind. The intuitive, unconscious mind, with its vast reservoir of imaginative connectors had been at work sometime during the hours of sleep.

It is personally exciting to discover that the more one puts this mental capacity to work and the more frequently one does it, the more one's creative skills improve.

If you want to improve your mental creative powers, exercise them!

Develop your "mental muscles." (These processes will be discussed further in the chapter entitled "The Care and Maintenance of the Brain.")

A second great practical value of fantasy is its use as a form of mental relaxation. Someone has said that one sign or characteristic of genius is the ability to return to childhood *at will.* In other words, it is essential that one be able, whenever necessary, to shift into that childlike state of simplicity and directness where one is in a play-world mode.

Hank Ketcham, the author of the cartoon character "Dennis The Menace" apparently has the ability to recapture that mental state for adult readers. It is a state of fresh curiosity, playfulness of the mind, freedom from fear, and freedom from suspicion which, in adult years, tends to block our capacity to see things openly and with fresh eyes. The biographies of many great scientific, musical, and artistic leaders are full of examples of this capacity for utter, childlike simplicity.

The degree of mental concentration attained by such persons is intense. If they do not acquire the disciplined ability to escape at will through fantasy, there would be danger of blowing out the "fuses" through mental fatigue.

The Rev. Dr. Culver H. Nelson[2] tells about an occasion years ago when he and Mrs. Nelson were invited to the home of Dr. Edgar J. Goodspeed for dinner. During a tour of the house, the young couple were shown into Goodspeed's large personal library. Having been the renowned translator of what became known as the Goodspeed New Testament and having also been Professor of Biblical and Patristic Greek at the University of Chicago's Divinity School, Rev. Goodspeed's library contained many priceless, old Bibles and related reference works. However, along one long wall was a collection of another sort: several thousand volumes of mystery stories. This was obviously Dr. Goodspeed's fantasy-stimulator — his mental relaxant and counterbalance to the serious work, which he also enjoyed.

That Goodspeed New Testament gives the following phrasing of St. Matthew 6:34:

So do not worry about tomorrow, for tomorrow will have worries of its own. Let each day be content with its own ills.

In focusing upon the present day, we are suggesting that one should not waste time or energy crossing all the rivers and mountains before one gets to them.

The powers of imagination are not just an enormous resource for us. Often, they are misused to exaggerate our anxieties. When that occurs, we tend to become uncertain about making decisions. The imaginary what-if's can immobilize us, or our fears may actually increase to the point of hysteria.

Instead of burning calories and energy needlessly on anxiety about all the disastrous things which *could* happen in the future, there is only a single question: What, if anything, can be done today to plan well for tomorrow? Perhaps one can only wait patiently for some extra piece to drop into place.

All right, then, one accepts that and waits.

You are not going to traverse all the roads up ahead, only one. There may be many options potentially open to you. Choices and plans need to be made in advance. Flexibility and contingency options may need to be built into your planning — at least to some degree. But when you reach the point of action, in some future present, you will only take one route.

It does no good at all to tell yourself over and over, "Don't worry, don't worry." The unconscious mind (where worries are exaggerated and what-if's are given extra urgency) does not respond to that kind of negative suggestion. It only responds to positive input.

The correct instruction for you to use is, "Think about this."

The command, "Stop thinking about that," or "Don't worry about that," does not enter the mind's control system as a positive suggestion. The unconscious mind is not programmed to accept the words "stop" or "don't." So, the only message that gets into your mental computer is a reinforcement of the words, "Worry about that," or "Think about that."

The result is more concentrated focus upon the very things about which you have been feeling anxious or disturbed.

This is one of the reasons why people are often so unsuccessful in their efforts to control their diets or to stop habits like smoking tobacco. In various ways they are giving suggestions to themselves phrased with negatives.

For instance, achieving a sugar-free diet is aided if one says things such as "I like sugar-free foods" or "Foods with sugar in them are oversweet and taste a little nauseous to me."

Trouble is ahead for the person who says, "I love to eat that cake or ice cream, but I can't have it." The control/motive centers of the mind pick up only the suggestions, "I love that" and "I have it."

Reducing the domination of old habits or nonproductive anxieties requires truer insights about ourselves, as well as long-term daily exercises in performance of the possible.

Worry disappears as confident action in the present moment becomes an increasingly enjoyable function.

That focus has its effects, also, upon the way we deal with the past.

Yesterday's Regrets

A sensitive, responsible person does not forget the past harm which may have been done because of one's earlier ignorance, thoughtlessness, or emotional limitations.

There are certain things one can do to make amends. However, this may not be possible in some instances.

Trying to repair a past wrong may do much more harm than leaving it alone.

There is a vast difference between amending and substituting. The first is an attempt to repair. The second is a trade-off. Very seldom can we compensate for past wrongs or neglected care by doing a later rerun. It can be even more harmful if we are merely trying to make ourselves feel better about past regrets.

Rather than do the wrong thing again, if we care about someone, it is better to bear the pain of the regret silently — perhaps only sharing it with an objective confidante. The pain, when it occurs in memory, is a healthy reminder that we are human. Remember, in part, love is the willingness to be hurt.

There are two positive things, beyond making amends, which we can always do:

1. We can stay alert for persons in trouble who may benefit from the newer insights which now enable us to perceive the causes of previous wrongs we once inflicted upon others.
2. In primarily focusing upon confident action today, we will find it is possible now to redeem some of the past by doing more caring, committed, intelligent things in the present.

If we botched some of the development needs when our own children were little, perhaps they are grown now and need to know we still love them, while recognizing their rights to independence.

If we failed to give adolescents the needed experience in making their own decisions and assuming the risks in smaller choices, there are other adolescents in school or summer jobs who might benefit from our assistance now.

If someone was unable or unwilling to assume needed responsibility when a child was born out of wedlock, there are now others in a similar situation who need the counsel or assistance from people who have been through the experience.

If separation from a mate left regrets about past actions, there are always others who are currently repeating the same kinds of mistakes. Experience can often lead one to find ways of putting that knowledge to constructive use. There are endless examples.

There are really only two limitations to the ways we can use the lessons of yesterday. One is time; the other is energy. But the significance of what we do is always in the quality of caring. We need to remind ourselves of that when the temptation comes to think of quantity and recognition as measurements of meaning.

How does the focus upon the present affect one's assumptions about a Power greater than oneself?

Assumptions About a Power Greater Than Oneself

As Maxwell points out in his perceptive book, Alcoholics Anonymous members may describe their spiritual experiences in terms ranging all the way from the natural to the supernatural. They may have been atheists, agnostics, theists, or believers in a variety of religions.[3] However, everyone who has closely and objectively observed A.A. members, from the psychiatrist, Dr. Harry M. Tiebout, in the 1940s to the present day, has noted a common process threading through all their experiences. This is an inner change which occurs as

1. egocentricity is deflated at a deep level,
2. one comes to a recognition that only some Power greater than self can restore the self, and
3. the act of trust, renewed one day at a time, produces a continuing spiritual growth beyond one's personal power.

An identical process is experienced by people who make good recoveries in similar groups, such as Gamblers Anonymous, Overeaters Anonymous, Narcotics Anonymous, etc.

It is also a process which anyone goes through whose life-crisis deflates egocentricity at a level so deep that a choice must be made between death and life.

The habit of daily trust in a greater Power than oneself creates a new level of consciousness. Without perceiving any specific plan or destiny, one senses a movement *with the Grain of the Universe.* Upon looking backward, one is soon amazed to perceive that beneficial changes are occurring within one's life — changes which are *beyond the power of the self.*

CHAPTER 4
IT IS BETTER TO PLAY THAN TO WORK

Life's crises often bring career crises: the need to find a job or to change one's job, the need to reassess one's work choices.

Obviously, these are difficult periods. But they illustrate the age-old lesson that the most difficult problems are often the ones that open the doors to our greatest opportunities.

However, there is usually much pain and adjustment between the loss and the gain. It is not easy to thread our way through the labyrinth of problems, conflicting advice, false starts, and abortive experiments to find the feasible and happy solution that fits us. In looking backward we can see that the crisis made possible a great opportunity, but the swamp of problems and frustrations we had to wade through to get there often tested our strength and abilities.

Many individuals have gone through such experiences. Five of the more common events that bring on a career crisis are 1) termination of one's job, 2) single parenthood, 3) recovery from major illness or accident, 4) square-peg-in-the-round-hole syndrome, and 5) realignment of life goal systems.

Termination of One's Job

Whenever a person is fired, permanently laid off, or loses the job through an organization change, there may be a need for a major shift in career direction. If a person is happy in the present work, and positions are available within other organizations, the job loss will probably cause only temporary inconvenience.

Terminations which signal the end of a career have become very common. One may have been partially forewarned by certain events, but hardly ever is there an inner preparation for the immense shock that one feels.

The English have an expressive word for this kind of event. When a person loses a job, it might be explained by saying, "I have been made redundant." The British usage is "redundant: unnecessary or unfit for a job." Obviously, the emotional shock of such a layoff, whatever it may be called, can be severe. Economic security and one's self-image may both be threatened.

The cause may have been a radical shift in business products or services. The event may have been triggered by the impersonal merger or sundering of large organization structures. Sometimes it is occasioned by an individual being promoted into job assignments which are ill-suited to aptitudes or personal preferences. There is seldom any one reason, but a combination of events that come together at some point in time. Unfortunately, some people are too slow in absorbing the news. They do not react soon enough to seek other employment before their personal resources are exhausted or overextended. This sort of delay can complicate the original problem and make it doubly or triply difficult to utilize the occasion for the development of new opportunities.

Single Parenthood Crises

A totally different kind of crisis may occur when a single homemaker finds it necessary to assume the dual roles of homemaker and home-provider.

One type of difficulty occurs for the person who has been away from a line of employment for some time. It may be necessary to take refresher courses. One may have to start at a lower level of compensation than one held on the last position, or to make some other adjustment temporarily, which will permit the management of the dual roles.

Another kind of problem besets a provider who, for the first time, must assume full homemaker duties also.

A third type of situation confronts an individual who simultaneously and temporarily has less than top health/energy levels.

It is important for individuals in any of these categories to secure information about appropriate community services and/or assistance for job retraining, work hours help with children, job placement, and/or health services.

Serious Illness or Accident Recovery

These crises may strike younger people, who have not previously held permanent jobs. But they more often affect older people who find that health recovery still leaves them without the ability to perform at the type of work for which they have previous skills.

Whatever causes the need for a vocational decision, there is a wide variety of resources for personal assistance. We will review several of the more useful ones later.

The Square-Peg-in-a-Round-Hole Syndrome

A problem which has not received the attention it deserves is what I call the square-peg-in-the-round-hole syndrome. In today's occupational world this frustrating problem is one of the reasons why many people suffer from what is called "burn out" on their jobs. Their aptitudes do not truly fit the work they do.

Unfortunately, many people would apparently rather endure their dissatisfactions and gripe about them, than go through the uncertainty and risk of attempting a change. This is understandable, especially when the compensation received from wages and fringe benefits has reached a level where one's pay is far more than could immediately be obtained from a new place of employment.

A person in middle years with heavy financial responsibilities may feel trapped between career frustrations and the prospect of accepting lower pay during an extended period of new training and building additional job skills.

But the long-term rewards in life satisfaction, not to mention greater financial security, may be so great that a shift in career should be seriously considered. Even though the immediate obstacles seem insurmountable, there are often more options and resources for change than one might perceive at first.

A Realignment of Life Values

A final cause of vocation change sometimes occurs in mid-career when there is a shift or realignment in one's life values.

For instance, an acquaintance in his early forties had been very successful as a partner in a medium-sized manufacturing company. He decided to switch careers and enter the Protestant clergy. After three years of graduate study at a theological seminary, he served as a pastor for a few years. Then, he had an opportunity to direct the fund-raising program for a church-related college. Because of his prior experience in business and finance, he was able to expand this institution and put it into a strong financial condition. He continued successfully in that career until his retirement.

A different kind of example demonstrates how frustration may lead to deep bitterness for a person who fails to adjust career values to fit reality.

From your childhood reading, you may recall "The Tale of Peter Rabbit" by an English author, Beatrix Potter, when she was a young girl. The story about Peter Rabbit, along with Flopsy, Mopsy, and Cottontail and their adventures in Mr. McGregor's garden became very popular and widely read. It was recognized, both in England and in the United States, as a classic children's story and made Miss Potter a loved and famous author throughout the English-speaking world.[1]

But, after middle life, she married an English landowner and went in heavily for the so-called respectability of the gentry class.

She grew violently ashamed of "The Tale of Peter Rabbit." She never allowed that name to be mentioned in her presence. Then, oddly, she became an expert in the art of shooting rabbits! A sad illustration of how important it is that we devote our energy happily to doing useful things which truly fit us.

Decision Making: Self-Assessment

In making any career choice or major job change the most important factor is assessing yourself and deciding what occupation fits you.

The place to start, of course, is to ask: What are the things I have found which do not fit me? What work have I done in the past that I dislike? Or, what kind of studies did I like best in school? What sort of avocational and recreational activities have I enjoyed most?

The answers to such questions are very good clues about the things that fit your personality, skills, and tastes.

There will be activities you identify as having been a cause of some dislike. In those instances, it will pay you to ask yourself further questions about what were the causes of the distaste. Was it simply the conditions under which you conducted the activity or the work? Or the personality of the individuals with whom you were associated? Were there things about the tasks or responsibilities, themselves, which you found disagreeable?

In the midst of an activity that you may have generally disliked, were there parts of it that you enjoyed? What were they? Perhaps it will help you to organize these likes and dislikes if you make written lists of them, giving a rank order to each list.

As you begin to focus upon those activities you have identified as enjoyable, try to avoid premature consideration of whether any of them would be financially rewarding. We often jump too quickly into the question of where there might be jobs available that pay well. We shall get to those considerations shortly, but initially it is vital to focus upon what truly fits you. What would be your useful, enjoyable activity, if you were completely free to choose? If these primary questions are not resolved, you are apt to find yourself right back in the same kind of frustrated situation you are trying desperately to escape.

In making such choices on several occasions, I have developed a useful game that helps me identify what would be a fun kind of work.

I have recommended the game to many people. It is very simple. You might call it "The Financially Independent Test." You suppose that you have an income for life from a trust fund which is adequate to provide all your essential living expenses, including inflation increases.

With this pretended security in hand, you then ask yourself this question, "Now, what kind of useful activity would I enjoy?" Try to envision a set of activities which would include all those things you have identified as enjoyable in your work, studies, and avocational experiences. After you have gotten the results from playing this game, you should have a rather good assessment of what kind of activities best fit your tastes and aptitudes.

If you already have some years of work experience in a field and enjoyed parts of it, there is no point in "throwing the baby out with the bath." If you can put together a new career into which past experience and skills fit, this is obviously preferable to an option that requires learning totally new skills.

Now, what resources are available to assist the actual decision making?

Decision Making: Resources

Vocational aptitude testing and counseling can be a valuable resource. This is a special branch of psychological testing.

Some people still shy away from the use of tests as a measurement of an individual's capacity and occupational interests. This resource has sometimes received a bad name because of two unfortunate circumstances.

First, popular articles about psychological testing have often failed to mention that a well-designed and well-administered group of tests measures a wide variety of abilities. The purpose of the test is to obtain a balanced, objective review of the many complex individual factors. In contrast, some popular articles attach too much importance to a single psychological measurement, such as a person's average IQ (Intelligence Quotient). In actuality, that average can be based upon eight to twelve separate scores from a person's IQ test — depending upon the test instrument being used.

The notion that one could predict probable success in a line of work from such an average, especially without administering a variety of other interest and skills tests is as full of holes as a piece of Swiss cheese. It would be like using the single measurement of a young person's height to assess whether the individual had the aptitude to learn and play basketball effectively. Height is important, but there are many other complex factors.

A second misunderstanding about aptitude testing is caused by a problem common to all professions. As in music, medicine, or social work, it is one thing to learn the techniques of the craft; it is something else to have the instincts for practice of the arts.

Like people trained in any other field, not all psychologists have the empathy and human relations experience needed for effective one-on-one work with individuals. They may do very well in the areas of research or statistical analysis. However, if such an individual is assigned to a position in vocational testing, too much reliance is apt to be placed upon test scores, rather than on a blending of personal observation and insights obtained in the interviewing process.

In spite of these drawbacks, the positive values of psychological testing are so great that they outweigh the minor inconvenience of seeking those professionals who have skills in the vocational counseling specialty.

You may be one of those individuals we call multiple aptitude persons. Some people in that category are able to find vocations that combine most of their major interests. Others can achieve life satisfaction through a combination of work, plus free-time hobbies that engage their remaining interests. Testing is especially helpful to such individuals.

Vocational aptitudes testing and counseling are available privately through individuals, groups of psychologists, out placement agencies, and some public vocational rehabilitation or employment departments.

A good place to start a search for such professional help is to make inquiry through graduate psychological departments of local universities. They would have information about places in your area where graduates have been employed.

In addition to testing and counseling, there are other kinds of information and help which will be useful, depending upon your own situation. Among these needs may be how to develop and follow through on a job interview list, how to conduct effective interviews, sources for specific job skills training and financing, lists of employers in your area, lists and descriptions of occupations, and how to prepare personal resumes.

Much of this information is available in public libraries of cities above 50,000 population. Several good self-help handbooks on job searching have been published in recent years, including those specifically written to aid the job searches of managerial and junior executive persons. Libraries contain data on names and addresses of local industries, listings of job classifications, and background information on future job opportunities. There are also listings on local health and welfare agencies.

Another good source of information about assistance for job training programs, vocational rehabilitation services, and day-care services is the central office of the United Fund or United Way.

If you are physically handicapped, you may wish to contact both the private and the public vocational rehabilitation services which make available certain job training experiences and job counseling.

There is another fairly new type of job exploration, which is being used by many career searchers who are not burdened with family financial responsibility.

Voluntary Service

Offered through a wide variety of organizations and available under many arrangements, contracts for voluntary service provide several advantages to a person choosing a vocational field.

One of the big problems a person usually faces in exploring a new field is having an opportunity to experience just what the work situation is like. If one is going into medicine, there will be opportunities through internship and residency to get work experience under supervision. Or, if a person is training for public school teaching, there are regularly scheduled programs of practice teaching. Many types of work, however, do not provide this sort of experience about how work is actually done nor how it feels to work with people already in the field.

In voluntary service a person finds opportunities to gain exposure to those experiences. Also, with a broad field one often has a chance to explore working conditions as they exist in several specialty occupations.

For instance, suppose one is interested in working as a naturalist or in environmental activities within a wilderness setting. A three-month summer assignment with the U.S. Forest Service or a wilderness organization may provide experience in a rather wide variety of tasks. One might be involved in anything from an archaeological dig to engineering problems of bridge construction in rough terrain.

Another example might be a six-month assignment to a health or welfare agency, where it would be possible to observe or participate in several medical or social work teams. One could see how such professionals work in that environment and observe the actual conditions surrounding several professionals in that setting.

At the same time, since one is in the role of volunteer, that role removes a person somewhat from the usual professional competitive pattern. So, the full-time professionals on the job are much more cooperative and inclined to share their insights with the volunteer worker. They will often be very open about discussing the organizational environment in which they are involved.

Another advantage of volunteer work is its openness to opportunities for work variety. Usually, in a regular paid job, a person is allotted into a particular assignment. Months or years may elapse before a person has a chance to function closely with individuals doing related tasks or other jobs within the organization. In the volunteer position, one is often asked to do bits and pieces, or whole projects, with a wide selection of full-time paid people. Thus, in a relatively short time one receives a feeling for not only different kinds of work available, but also how these relate to the total objectives and policies of the organization in which they are done.

A further advantage is the great freedom one has to move about and communicate with people of various status levels in an organization. Often it is possible to observe firsthand the manner in which managers, policy-makers, and professionals relate to one another. In the workplace there may be undue stress or feelings of competition that interfere with job objectives or promotion advancement. The volunteer, who keeps his or her own counsel, is in an ideal spot to observe these things and to make mental note of possible disadvantages that may be inherent in certain organization structures or in certain types of work.

The volunteer may consider that the observed behavior is usual for this sort of occupation. If one's aptitudes fit the career, the stresses will probably not be bothersome. However, the volunteer service will give forewarning to expect such pressures.

If a volunteer contract extends over a six-month or a year period there will, of course, be more access to the inside functions of an organization than during shorter contracts. In any case, a person who is willing to work hard and is interested in learning will have greater access to inside information than would any paid employee doing similar tasks for the same length of time.

A final advantage in these options is the possibility of acquiring individual mentors — people whose advice and contacts may be very useful in a job search.

At the same time, a volunteer is not under any special job pressure to choose that field as a career. Consequently, a person has a great deal of freedom to consider various options and to think through the decisions one must make.

Some examples of organizations offering this type of temporary service are

The U.S. Forest Service Volunteer Program, U.S. Department of Agriculture, Washington, D.C.

The Volunteers in Parks Program of the National Park Service; or The National Volunteer Coordinator, Division of Refuge Management, U.S. Fish and Wildlife Service; both under the U.S. Department of Interior, Washington, D.C.

Any large environmental group, such as Sierra Club, the Wilderness Society, or National Audubon Society; various Hiking Societies that offer working vacations; Religious and church-related organizations, which offer a wide variety of volunteer opportunities, such as overseas teaching, welfare work, geriatric work, and poverty-area service — both urban and rural.

Service agreements vary, extending anywhere from a few weeks to as long as a year. They usually provide basic living expenses while working. The year-long contracts are usually given with provision of room and board with a monthly stipend for miscellaneous expenses. One needs to explore the conditions in each situation to determine whether the type of work and the financial arrangements are such that an individual can manage the experience.

Practical Tips for Survival

A person who has family responsibility will usually not have the luxury of being able to explore job options through voluntary service.

If one has a job or if one or both spouses are working, even though the work may have some distasteful features, it is usually better to continue with that arrangement for a time, rather than seeking other interim types of support.

If the former jobs have been lost, it will probably be necessary to seek what might be called a survival job, or a series of them, to meet basic needs. In that case, one should make a strong effort to take a positive attitude toward oneself and the reality being faced.

This is no time to let yourself slip into the common trap of thinking, "I failed to keep my job; therefore, I must be a 'failure.' "

A person is not a "failure" because "success" does not always come. Sometimes one loses, and sometimes one wins. But these events are not the things which make one a "loser" or a "winner." Those are artificial terms that publicity people use when they "manufacture" celebrities.

These are labels. They are not YOU.

So, if you have lost a job and you need a little ego-boosting, see your clergy person or a counselor or an older mentor who believes in you.

But do not attach labels to yourself. People cannot be properly designated as successes or failures! There are only some of us who are *becoming* a little better or *becoming* a trifle worse today than we were yesterday.

Usually, most of us can reverse many of these processes anytime, BY THE SIMPLE EFFORT OF CHOOSING TO DO SO.

In survival jobs, one should attempt to learn everything possible from those experiences. For instance, at one point in my own career the only opening available was in a bookkeeping position. To put it mildly, bookkeeping is several steps removed from my primary interests, but it was a living. So, I decided to invest a small amount of money and effort in attending night school to learn about basic accounting principles.

Several years later, I found myself in an administrative position where, among other departments, I was to supervise the head of a small accounting group. The elementary training and experience as a bookkeeper was helpful as background for proper understanding of the accountant's problems, whose technical knowledge was obviously far in excess of my own.

There are other financial possibilities that you would do well to consider during the interim period.

First, you will naturally want to get decisions made and get relocated in a permanent career as soon as possible. But do not let this feeling of impatience short-circuit the time necessary for planning and preparation. Try to equip yourself as well as you can for each succeeding step in the process of making a new beginning.

Second, since your family obligations and training needs will probably stretch available income to the limit, pay special attention to working out a budget of your needs, and try to stick with it. Remember, in our present affluent society most people have a tendency to get their wants confused with their needs. Budget austerely without impairing health and long-term survival.

Third, when you are working through this kind of crisis, remember that family help from those who know you well may surprise you. It is important to remain independent, but it is also a sign of maturity to be willing to accept help graciously from those who truly want to give it.

Fourth, you do not need to see the end of your course in order to make a beginning or to follow immediate steps in your plan. Take things one day, or one "now," at a time. Focus upon making each choice a good choice, which you will be happy about. Get your satisfactions from solving today's problems today.

Remember, marathon races are won by those who pace themselves and who learn to breathe steadily, evenly, and deeply. Don't get yourself into a sweat.

In connection with job training, job choices, and job searching, there are four additional tips which may be useful:

1. In training, when possible, tap into rehabilitation programs, industrial scholarships, or tuition aid plans.
2. In seeking initial positions, it is advisable to look for places where a combination of working and learning is available.
3. Seek the advice of older, experienced mentors. Avoid cluttering your mind with advice from people whose own track records are mediocre.
4. When you have decided upon the type of career you wish to enter and have the background to begin, do not overlook the option of finding someone who can be sold on hiring you for such an assignment.

A Final Word From One Who Has Been There

Let's look ahead to the time when you have gotten settled in your new career. Since the enjoyment level of doing what fits you will be high, you have gotten very good at the work. You will begin to receive offers of promotion in your field.

Here is a danger point.

In considering any promotion it will be essential that you *stick with the original criteria* you used in locating your new career. There are three questions that should be resolved, and they should be answered *in the following sequence:*

1. Does it fit me?
2. Will it give more opportunities for learning and growth?
3. Would it pay a sufficient amount?

If you start to consider pay or status ahead of the first two questions, you will begin to get into trouble. You will soon find yourself in the kind of situation where your work is no longer play.

No amount of pay or status can make up for that loss.

CHAPTER 5
WHY DO I HURT,
AND WHY AM I HERE?

A friend wrote about her heart surgery. While under anesthetic, her heart stopped and was restarted. Then a coronary artery bypass was completed. Sometime during these procedures, she also suffered a stroke, which caused some paralysis of her left arm and leg.

Three months afterwards, she had regained enough leg movement to discard crutches, and sufficient arm use to answer correspondence on her typewriter.

Rejoicing in what seemed like a miraculous restoration of life, she wrote, "Which leads one to interesting philosophical thoughts: Why didn't I die? What am I here to do? It sort of makes everything different."

Times of critical illness or life-threatening accident raise questions about the meaning of one's existence. We ponder the physical limitations within which we exist. We make comparisons between what we are and what we once were. We tend to pause and look at ourselves with fresh understandings. Questions about our life-directions and our place in the universe often come to mind. During less critical periods of our lives we may tend to take the answers to such questions for granted, assuming that there must be answers, even though we have not bothered to ask the questions!

What about our place in the universe? What about our limitations?

Humankind is vastly superior mentally to other life forms on the planet.

Physically, however, all life forms have many limitations. A comparison among ourselves, other mammals, and some insects is not flattering. As adults, we cannot run as well as the horse. We cannot jump as well as the kangaroo. Our strength is feeble when compared to that of the elephant, the bear, or the whale. Our teeth are in some ways inferior to those of the wolf; our sense of hearing does not compare favorably to that of the deer, nor to that of the dog, which is said to be capable of hearing the heart beat of a person fifteen feet away. In comparison with insects, few of us can leap, proportionate to size, more than 1/100 as high as the flea. Our single-lens eyes lack the peripheral scope of even the common housefly.

Now, these physical limitations do not worry us. We accept them as part of our normal equipment.

The limitations that do bother us are those which set us, or one of our family members, apart by birth from other humans, or those which come upon us because of accidents, illnesses, and advancing age.

We are not frustrated by those limitations that are common to the human species during the full power of our mature years. But we suffer pain and anger when we see a loved person born into the world with a physical or mental deficiency.

According to the *1973 Birth Defects: Atlas and Compendium,*[1] there were then 842 birth defects which had been observed and described! Of course, many of these are overlapping and/or interrelated in individual occurrences. And many of the conditions are relatively rare. But almost everyone knows of families and individuals who have experienced the trauma of such limitations.

When they occur, the people involved are not dealing with statistics. They are confronted with pain, anguish, struggle, and the need to cope with the situation.

The *Atlas* does not include such disabilities as paralysis of an arm caused by injury during the process of birth, nor persons who are born with mental capacity low enough to interfere seriously with later adult capability.

Most of us are fortunate enough to get into this world and grow toward adulthood with a fairly good mental-physical set of equipment. But somewhere along the way, a disabling accident or illness strikes some of us. It can be painfully difficult to lose a function or physical skill. One's first reaction is usually one of disbelief. The second feeling is of anger, or denial.

Most people have tried to imagine what it would be like to lose the use of a limb or one's eyes. But it is very difficult to "fill the shoes" of someone whose muscles cannot move the feet or to visualize the darkness of one whose optic nerve no longer transmits the signal of light to the brain.

Another type of disability occurs with advancing years, when various parts of the anatomy begin to show marked decline in endurance, strength, and performance.

Unlike "The Wonderful One-Horse Shay" described in Oliver Wendell Holmes' poem, the parts of the human body do not age uniformly. In one person, perhaps the skin will be the first organ to show signs of aging. It may lose some of its elasticity and healthy tone, while the internal organs of the same individual may remain quite strong. Another older person's veins and arteries can be aging more rapidly than other parts of the anatomy. This great circulatory system of bodily plumbing may have become quite brittle in some older persons. Any injury or unusual stress can produce extra risks and may complicate recovery when the person suffers from other illnesses.

Slowly, or rapidly in some instances, muscles lose their size and strength. The sheath material that encloses each tendon and muscle unit becomes more brittle. These gristle-like sheaths may have small, painful ruptures when quick movements are required in an emergency, such as a threatened fall. Hearing can become impaired, while sight remains quite good, or vice versa.

Just because these gradual disabilities are a usual part of aging does not mean they are necessarily easy for a person to accept. In fact, those who have enjoyed relatively good health during previous years of their lives are apt to have the most difficulty accepting and adjusting themselves to the effects of aging. Perhaps their prior good health may have reinforced the illusion that they are somehow immune to the limitations of mortality.

At any age, from youth to the older years, it irritates us when legs that once took us easily across mountains or tennis courts must be aided by walkers or canes. We have a sense of frustration when hands that once whipped up a cake or broke kindling sticks to build a camp fire or sewed a straight seam or gripped an axe handle become deformed or weakened.

When any of the five senses become less reliable or we lose some of our physical strength and skills, we experience a feeling of acute loss. We are frustrated. And, if we do not begin to deal promptly and effectively with our frustration, we become angry, guilty, or resentful.

Our anger may show itself in various ways. It may express itself through increased irritation with other people or the circumstances of life around us. We sometimes make *ourselves* the scapegoat — developing massive amounts of self-pity, or self-blame, on the assumption we are guilty of something for which we are being punished.

For many individuals, the first and most difficult question is, "Why did this disability happen to me?" or "Why did this undeserved limitation befall the person I love?"

We often hear it said, "Why did God permit this?"

Such a question raises an issue which has long troubled sensitive people. It is asked when natural disasters — floods, volcanic eruptions, tidal waves, or earthquakes — wipe out large numbers of people.

In the United States several hundred people died in a hurricane that hit the East Coast on September 14, 1944, and during one of our worst blizzards on record in February 1958 more than 500 people died in the northeastern part of the country.[2]

Compared with other parts of the world and other times, we have been fortunate to have escaped many great disasters that have occurred.

As recently as November 12, 1970, between 300,000 and 500,000 persons lost their lives in the Ganges River Delta area of what is now Bangladesh as a result of a cyclone and tidal wave in that low-lying ground.

In the spring of 1887 the Yellow River overflowed and an estimated 1,500,000 persons died in China.[3]

As a result of an innundation in Holland in the year 1421 about 100,000 people lost their lives and, again, in 1530 the dikes failed, causing the death of 400,000 people.

The greatest disaster of recorded history was the Black Death (bubonic plague), which began in 1348. Before it was over, 25,000,000 people died in Europe, about one-third the population at that time on the continent. The island populations of Cyprus and Ireland were totally wiped out. More than half the people in Italian cities such as Florence, Siena, and Pisa lost their lives. A man in Siena wrote after burying five of his children, "No one wept for the dead, because everyone expected death himself."

The plague altered every aspect of human life in ways which profoundly influenced Western thought and our entire culture to the present day.

Some people adopted an "eat, drink, and be merry philosophy." Others took the view that the Black Death must have been sent by God to punish humanity for its sinful ways. This response can be seen in literary works, such as Petrarch's writings, and the Latin poem, "Dies Irae" (Days of Wrath), which talks about the final extinction of the universe. Francisco Traini's painting *Triumph of Death* depicts a scene of horror, warning people to repent before sudden death seizes them.[4]

Out of this same period, however, came an increasing influence of the Franciscan Order, which was based upon the ideas and example of St. Francis of Assisi, who found evidence of God's goodness everywhere. He expressed those views in his famous song, *Canticle of the Sun.*

In more modern times the cost and destructive potential of great wars are raising the same issue in a different form. Since individuals do not feel they have any real control over whether the risk of atomic annihilation may become a reality, many people ask, "Would God permit this. And if so, why?"

But for most of us, the issue of bad things happening to ostensibly decent people comes closest home on occasions when disabilities are brought to us through individual illness or accident.

Let us see whether we can find some answers to those situations. If we can, perhaps we shall have moved far toward resolving the personal question of how we may view suffering and pain in our understanding of God.

First, let us take a look at some of the ways people have tried to explain personal disaster when it strikes them, from whatever source or cause it comes.

As we have noted, when floods, earthquakes, typhoon, or other forces of nature occur in heavily populated areas, the loss of human life can be enormous. The same can be said of situations where diseases are not yet within our control.

To some degree, we may alter events in our environment to make them more safe and more fair to ourselves and others. Examples are seen in our discoveries and successful remedies for bubonic plague, scarlet fever, malaria, and polio.

Humane people feel the responsibility to make the earth safe, certain, and fair to other persons. But there are practical limits to *how* safe, *how* certain, and *how* fair we can expect life to be for ourselves and others.

The reality is that our earth is a dangerous place. Every individual has to assume a large share of the risks in one's own life. From the moment we are born we start dying, and we are engaged in constant vigilance to avoid disabilities along the way. We are residing in a place wherein many events are unsafe, uncertain, and unfair to us — often *to a massive degree!*

One approach is to seek answers to painful happenings beyond our control by suggesting explanations in religious terms. When disease or an accident causes disability or the sudden death of a child, we sometimes adopt one of the ideas used by people exposed to the Black Death. We suggest the disease is a punishment of God for some presumed evil of people.

The notion is illogical that health and freedom from accidents are rewards from God for good behavior or that sickness and natural disasters are punishments for bad people. If this were so, how could one explain the fact that birth defects, broken backs, multiple sclerosis, arthritis, blindness, deafness, various types of paralysis, and an endless list of other disabling conditions are statistically so evenly distributed? Gangsters, priests, politicians, murderers, embezzlers, mothers-of-the-year, or assorted saints and sinners all receive approximately a proportionate share of such ailments!

However, there are deeper questions.

Question: If God is good and God loves us, why should such a deity permit so many bad things to happen to so many apparently decent people? And why does such a God permit so many beneficial events, such as rainfall, sunshine, and prosperity, to benefit scoundrels who are indecent to the rest of us?

Question: Does God inflict bad events upon people to encourage the development of strength and character?

The difficulty when such queries are pursued is that they are not answerable. Trying to answer them assumes that the human mind, if it works hard enough, may discover the ultimate essence and purpose of that reality we describe as consciousness. But human inquiries have consistently encountered blank walls or only partial solutions whenever these questions are pursued.

When we ask why we are on this planet, what is our purpose here, or when we inquire about the goodness and badness we experience, the questions are usually prompted because of two concerns. Either we are philosophically curious, or we have encountered some personal pain which needs an explanation.

If our approach is philosophical, it leads us to the question, "What is the purpose of the universe and mankind's place in it?"

If our search begins because we are puzzled by the reason for suffering or personal disaster, and if we have been exposed to religious beliefs (as most of us have), then we ask, "If God is both good and all-powerful, why is evil permitted?"

Regardless of which motive prompts our search, we come eventually to one of two alternatives.

One possibility is that God probably does not exist, and there is no purpose in the universe, at least none our present data and level of intelligence can discern. The other alternative is that the existence of evil can only be explained if we assume that God is either severely self-limited, or that God is part of the universal process of growth and creativity.

Neither of these alternatives is very attractive as a basis for everyday living if one looks at them honestly and realistically. However, there are many people who continue to search diligently through philosophy and religion for some explanation. So, they continue to re-explore the alternatives, perhaps for years, hoping that they may find something they missed previously — a clue that will provide them with a simple and satisfying answer.

For instance, the story of Job is a book-length parable about a man who lost his wealth, reputation, family, and health. Job complains at length to God. Then his so-called friends, Eliphaz, Gildad, and Zophar, come to him. A long series of conversations take place about the possible reasons for Job's afflictions.

The dialogues conclude with a conversation between God and Job.

Like many persons in real life who have searched deeply for the reasons why evil things happen to decent people, Job's story ends with his statement:

"But I have spoken of great things
which I have not understood,
things too wonderful for me to know."

Typical also of this kind of search is the philosophical inquiry of the prophet, Habakkuk, also recorded in the Old Testament.

The question asked here of God is, why are evil, marauding armies permitted to overcome people who are more righteous than the invaders?

Again, the inquirer can find no logical answer. Habakkuk can only retain his belief in God by making the affirmation of faith that even if the countryside lies totally ravaged and desolate, "Yet I will exult in the Lord. . . ."

One can search through the massive philosophical and religious libraries of the world without finding answers more satisfying than these.

Nevertheless, searching minds continue to ask the deep questions: Why are we here? Is there any rational answer to the nature of a deity who seems to coexist with evil in the universe?

Also, in science today the most striking fact may be that the same sense of mystery remains. Through deeper exploration of our physical universe, we have continually hoped to find clues about the meaning of human life. But throughout recorded history, we have been unable to penetrate the veil of mystery and awe. Whenever we thought we had gotten to a boundary, someone with a new instrument, or a combination of techniques, opened a further vista for exploration.

And then, in this century, science has opened doors to many new mysteries, not the least of which is the acknowledgment that consciousness may have a central role not envisioned in the older Newtonian universe.

For instance, George Wald, winner of the Nobel Prize for Physiology of Medicine, made some interesting comments in a paper presented at the 1982-1983 winter meeting of Orbis Scientiae in Miami, Florida.[5] As reported in *Science News,* he said:

Perhaps instead of consciousness being a late evolutionary development, it, instead, was there all the time and formed the material universe — bringing out life and specific forms of consciousness.

Another irony is that the discoveries of modern physics have suddenly made it necessary for science to become more humble. No longer can science be so certain in predicting the future. To predict one must know the present, but the present is not knowable. In trying to know the present universe, scientists have found they unavoidably change it. (The very method of examination — light, for example — may alter a subatomic particle.)[6]

So, we still have the question of what is the role of humankind in the universe? The great advances of science will not give us the answer, since science has now discovered things which are not understandable through scientific method. The mystery of why we are here, and where is "here" remains with us.

So, what is the proper, the productive, solution?

There is a spiritual alternative which totally bypasses the dead ends, the dogmas, the frustrations, and the limitations we have been describing.

Yet, this solution is so utterly simple that it often eludes us.

"Why?" is the wrong question.

Humankind has never found a satisfactory answer to it. Another problem is that the search often escalates our innate egocentricity.

Seeking to find the answers to "why I am here" or "what is my ultimate purpose on earth" can not only lead to narrow dogmatism or disillusionment, but that pathway is also an elaborate ego-trip. The question assumes that my sense of meaning depends upon locating some way in which I am a special, unique person apart from other persons, or at least apart from other persons who disagree with my views. The question assumes that finding *the* answer will occur within a personal self-discovery process.

Contributing to these egocentric influences is the great, subversive, driving human need to escape from one's own mortality.

We all share in a common problem related to our human condition. On one hand, we are capable of dreaming and fulfilling great and noble dreams. We can create music, art, ideals, poetry, philosophy, and socially useful devices.

On the other extreme, we become ill, we die, and then enter the biodegradable processes. We bleed, we discharge body wastes, are capable of brutalizing and killing one another. And, at best, we are constantly reminded that we are limited and mortal.

So, our seeking to answer the *why question* is largely a response to the need for self-importance and a need for a sense of immortality pictured as egocentric survival. That search is the ultimate escape route from those features about ourselves which we would like to deny and reject — the things about ourselves which we despise. Yet, the search never brings us to a happy acceptance of ourselves nor to the ability to be at home within ourselves or the universe.

Instead of "why," the correct question we should ask is, *"How do I live?"*

If we surrender enough of our egocentricity, we can focus upon that question one day at a time. Then, what seems like a miracle begins to take over our personalities. This is a pathway which universally works for individuals of many religions or philosophical systems. Certainly, however, for people in the Christian tradition the "how" approach is an expression of its most profound insights.

As one clergyman has pointed out, people have long been occupied with the question, "Why is there suffering and evil in the world?" But the proper question we should address, the one to which Jesus suggests we turn is not why but how. For instance, *"How* shall I suffer?"[7]

The first radical change which occurs when we shift attention primarily to the how of living is a special emphasis upon the present moment. This does not imply that we stop planning for the future, but we begin to plan without undue concern for our self-importance, or asking ourselves whether the task at hand has enduring value.

One has come to a realization that the ultimate — the eternal — meaning of one's efforts is not within one's grasp. Planning has to be confined to the tasks at hand, not extended to concern about whether one is in charge of everything — whether one is in a position to play God.

CHAPTER 6
COPING WITH LIMITATIONS: HOW?

Basic human traits have changed very little for thousands of years. But the inventive ways we discover to cope with our environment are varied, and often surprising. We keep changing the face of planet Earth (not always beneficially), and we alter our ideas and customs.

Over the centuries we have evolved different ways of dealing with suffering, pain, and limiting circumstances. For example, in the older Eskimo culture, where physical mobility was a necessity in coping with the harsh, frigid weather, there was one option when old age or disabilities reached a certain stage. The person would simply walk out into the frozen wildnerness and not return. In that environment it was a practical, if harsh, way to deal with physical incapacity.

In milder climates societies were able to sustain more disabled persons as useful members within the community. But it has only been possible through modern treatment and rehabilitative devices that large numbers of physically limited persons could survive and contribute substantially to their societies. They, and we all, have gained much as a result.

The degree to which we respond creatively to physical limitations depends upon four things. The first is our mental, emotional, and spiritual attitude toward the limitation. The second is the inventiveness and persistence we use in developing methods for coping with the problem. Then, there is the availability of medical and rehabilitation services. And, finally, the degree of family and peer group understanding is often crucial.

These are all interrelated. With the possible exception of rehabilitation services, the list applies to any type of crisis. The mental, emotional and spiritual responses of persons to pain and crisis are of utmost importance. If these adjustments are made in the most creative way, amazing things will happen. If we become inept, sour, or fear-ridden, then other factors cannot make up for those negatives.

From our culture, we have inherited four patterns of response to shock and painful experiences. They can be labeled a) stoicism, b) fatalism, c) hedonism, and d) resignation. There is now another method which society has begun to utilize on a large scale. We might call it the chemical response.

We often combine two or more of these approaches. Each of the methods has some advantages, but each also has severe limitations. If we take time to examine them, someone may be helped to avoid the futility of choosing one or more of these common options.

After we have looked briefly at each of the five, we will describe in detail a sixth approach, which was suggested in the preceding chapter. It has been proven in practice to be the best and most creative way to deal with human limitations.

The *stoical* response to unpleasant and painful experiences originated with a philosophy of the ancient Greeks. Ideally, to be strong meant that one did not display one's inner feelings. Those with tough human fiber were expected to endure much pain or discomfort, if need be. They were taught to continue with the business at hand as though there were no serious, personal problems.

Modern psychological studies have informed us that this view is only one side of the coin. As we know today, when one consistently takes the stoical stance, the initial problem is often compounded, since it is suppressed. The pain continues and may fester under the surface until the side effects can become even more disabling than the original limitation.

This does not mean that it is desirable for a person to wipe out all the restraints of privacy. It does mean that there are occasions when, and trusted persons with whom, the sharing of painful experiences can help us restore our sense of balance and objectivity.

The stoical method works best when the pain or problem is of short duration. Then, there may be value in minimizing the feeling of distress. One can often function normally without attracting unwanted attention until the problem rights itself or the pain subsides.

If a person can cope without the need for assistance from others, there may be value to one's self-esteem. Or, to put it another way, an adult person does not scream for help when a whisper will do, nor seek assistance when a moment of self-examination would reveal the injury was obviously short-lived and minor.

Akin to stoicism is the approach of considering the affliction to be a result of fate. *Fatalism* has often been used by people who have a firm faith that all events are predestined, or preordained, by God. What will happen, happens. One's whole life is laid out in detail from birth. A person plays out the part, as the scenes unfold. There is no need to ask why. Events of all sorts are simply one's fate. Pain and pleasure are meted out according to the plan; and, it is often thought, the balance for each individual will be established in the afterlife.

If one can accept and believe that life is constructed in this manner, there may be some degree of comfort in the belief. But there is little room, or need, for any kind of innovative, creative, or challenging response.

Another response to suffering is *hedonism*. It is popularly described as "eat, drink and be merry." To carry it off for any length of time usually requires a fair degree of financial independence! Eating, drinking, and partying on a large scale are expensive. Also, they are most enjoyably done in the company of other revelers, and that involves playing host some of the time.

The approach is one way of distracting attention from one's pain, at least temporarily. Long-term, truly satisfying adjustments are not generally found in this route. Like stoicism, the partying panacea is only useful as a short-term means of getting by until one can collect one's wits and get set for some relaxed, serious thought about one's problem.

At the other extreme is *resignation*. It takes several forms.

If one is provided with a caretaker, such as a loving mother, or a paid house sitter, it is possible, for instance, for a partially paralyzed young person to remain semipassive until the loving person dies, or the money runs out.

Another form of resignation is to be quite active in work or vocation, but avoid other activities which one feels are too strange or threatening.

For over thirty years, until she died, a friend supported herself with a sedentary occupation that could be conducted from her home. She wanted very much to travel. But her physical disability was used as an excuse for not becoming involved in the uncertainties and unfamiliar chores of travel, which she had avoided during earlier years of even less handicap.

All of her friends tried, without success, to get her started with some short tours. As the years went by, she slid further into a mood of resignation. If anything, she wanted more and more to travel, but knew she had lost the will to risk the strangeness of it. The thought of travel now terrified her!

A more subtle form of resignation occurs when a person is forced by circumstance to accept one limitation, but then expands that orbit to include one or more things which could clearly be undertaken. For instance, a high school graduate accepted a semiskilled job at a large company. Shortly after employment, he was badly burned in an industrial accident. After extended treatment, psychotherapy, and numerous skin graft surgeries, he finally recovered his health but had visible scars from some of the burns. He was offered an opportunity through rehabilitation funding to attend college, but refused. Apparently, he preferred to continue in a low-paying, low-visibility job, rather than aspire to a good chance of more fulfilling work and independence.

The fifth major response pattern is the *chemical* one. Certain native plants, as well as ethyl alcohol, have long provided the means to endure or escape from the chronic pains of living. In our modern chemical age, the availability and the variety of nonprescription drugs has tended to increase such use. Perhaps the fact that many of them are now illegal also adds to the excitement of use by persons who find it painful to cope with parts of society. Certainly, illegality indirectly increases prices to levels where production, distribution, and promotion become a way of life for both users and persons in a huge underground industry.

The other vast market, that of prescription drugs as a means of sedating our aches and pains, can be a great boon to many of us when they are properly prescribed by a physician. For instance, many arthritis sufferers would be far less mobile if inflammation and pain could not be controlled with medication.

The borderline between taking drugs, including alcohol, to cope or endure, and taking them to the point of developing dependency or alcoholism may sometimes be a very thin line. Freedom from pain or emotional trauma through such means is not a substitute for inner peace of mind and vocational adjustment.

The logical choice between these alternatives may not be a feasible option for some persons. When body chemistry and/or psychological patterns predispose individuals to becoming compulsively dependent, chemical assistance may add a fatal illness to the problem which originally caused a life crisis.

If you need to use prescription drugs for long periods to cope with pain, the danger signal is when the pain is not increasing, but your sense of need for the medication is growing. You should certainly then ask your doctor for second opinion consultation from a physician with special knowledge of chemical dependencies.

We have mentioned briefly five responses to pain and physical limitations: stoicism, fatalism, hedonism, resignation, and chemical aids to coping.

There is a sixth method, which is related to the life and teachings of Jesus. This response to experiences of pain and physical limitations is not focused upon asking, "Why did this happen?" or "What is its purpose?"

Instead, the entire mental concern is put upon the *immediate* question, "How can this experience be *used* constructively."

Jesus actually said nothing directly about coping with physical limitations or impairments. Oh, certainly, he healed the lame and the sick. He had compassion. But notice in the Gospels that nothing is said about the physical problems of the aging, or persons with severed limbs, or fading hearing, or bad teeth, or loss of the sense of equilibrium, or the crippling effects of arthritis. Yet, we know all of these have been common for thousands of years. Living with these kinds of limitations on a daily basis simply did not seem to be crucial matters for Jesus. He was a normal, healthy young person, who had not yet experienced any physical handicap, as far as we know from the Gospels' record.

However, he did speak indirectly to these problems within his teaching and through his example. It is in the matters he considered primary that one finds a positive approach to pain, disaster and human suffering.

First, Jesus said that it is not food, nor clothing, nor physical circumstances which determine the *quality or the function* of our lives. The functions of love, of giving oneself, of commitment to his Way should be our focus, according to Jesus. Specific skills, accomplishment, physical powers are not the summary of what makes one a whole person.

A second directive comes from an implication of this first principle, namely, that Jesus' approach to all of life's circumstances was for one to ask, "How can I use this experience for God?" This event, this joy, this pain, this experience I have had today — how can I use it to express creative love?"

He seemed to suggest the following practical steps:

Focus upon doing something you can do (today) rather than thinking about things you are unable to do (at the moment).

Focus upon giving your life to others, and you will find that more abundant life is given to you.

Share the little you have, and your *little* will become *much* in the benefit of others.

In contrast, anxiety about material possessions, preoccupation with one's limitations or one's future will blind a person to the opportunities to do and improve the many things he or she is capable of doing. One will also become blind to the best experiences of sunsets, falling rain, and real communication.

Accept yourself, Jesus seems to say, limited though you are, and your life will become open to more abundance.

Those events which seem to be bad fortune — the circumstances that we commonly label as disaster, or pain, or handicaps are, in reality, grist for the mill of our daily actions. For those who choose this approach to suffering and limitation, there are no truly "good" or "bad" events. There are only times when we *use* those events, or times when we momentarily forget to follow Jesus' suggestions.

When we forget, we find ourselves *used by,* or *abused by,* events.

He also seems to suggest that we should 1) learn to be comfortable in accepting our limitations, 2) recognize that we can love someone and still express irritations to that person, and 3) unburden ourselves of the need to prove our own perfection.

Those who are familiar with the Gospels will remember the scenes at the Mount of Olives and the Garden of Gethsemane. The Apostle Peter told Jesus that even if all the other disciples deserted him, certainly he, Peter, would never do so.

Jesus is reported as responding, "This very night you will deny me three times."

This conversation suggests that Jesus said, in effect, "Don't push yourself so hard, Peter. Just accept the fact that you have a breaking point. You have limitations, like everyone else. But I love you, nevertheless."

A little later, he returned to the disciples after praying privately and found them asleep. In irritation, he said, "Could you not watch one hour?" This happened three successive times. Yet, Jesus showed no sign of rejecting them. He accepted and loved them. He wanted them to accept themselves, to accept one another, and to love one another, even though there might be times when they were irritated and limited.

The first step toward a use of physical limitations is to accept them, not necessarily to expect that they will be removed by some spiritual or medical miracle. Then, one needs to focus upon what one *can* do, rather than upon what one *cannot* do at the moment.

When personal disaster strikes, the best antidote is to get busy immediately concentrating on how to make constructive use of the experience. Establishing that habit early is a great tool in avoiding destructive emotions such as self-pity, resentment, false guilt, and depression.

Also, in focusing exclusively upon how to use one's painful experience, another benefit is soon noticed. Rather soon one begins to experience a sense of achievement and inner elation. As time passes on, enJOYment seems to become a more constant state. Questions about, "Why," become unimportant. One is simply too busy, and too fulfilled, through focusing upon "How," to be concerned with unanswerable riddles.

This hyper-level of experiencing life is not attained, however, without overcoming certain hurdles. Those who recover well from painful crises seem to do so through a process of growth, which includes such steps as

1. enlargement of both curiosity and a sense of humor,
2. admission and acceptance of the problems, and
3. willingness to accept help while learning to walk alone.

People who overcome personal deprivation or pain are often credited with exercising extraordinary willpower or courage. That does not tally with personal experiences.

In the long haul, it is far more important that a person cultivate a fierce curiosity to see how much one can do in the face of obstacles. Coupled with this trait, one needs a large capacity for a sense of humor. By that is meant cultivating the ability to laugh at oneself to see the humorous side of the plight one has gone through or is working one's way out of. If those two characteristics can be retained, developed and blended together, a habitual attitude toward the situation is established. It is a healthy, resilient, joyful attitude.

A second factor in coping, or effectively using one's difficulty, is the honest admission and acceptance of the problem. Whenever one is confronted with a serious or traumatic personal tragedy or limitation, putting the emotions back in order requires, at some point, a release of grief. There comes a time, often in the privacy of one's room at night, when one must weep for oneself. If the problem is a disability, there needs to be one time when the fact is faced that, "I am a cripple" or "I have lost my hearing" or "My face is disfigured." If one has lost a mate, a similar time of grief and acceptance needs to occur.

Nowadays we refer to this as doing one's "grief work." Better than in yesteryears, we have learned to recognize the need to release grief when there is a severe family or personal loss of any kind. We no longer think that tears are a sign of weakness. Nature provides us with the means to grieve constructively. And we are less afraid today to use this pressure release valve.

In certain minor life limitations, the adjustment may sometimes be delayed longer than when we face a major disability. There are some younger persons who delay or avoid getting fitted with needed glasses. Or, older persons who continue to miss out on many conversations because they cannot accept that wearing a hearing aid would be helpful.

A third step in recovering from crisis and limitations is that of learning to accept help when needed. There will even be times when assistance must be sought. If one's need is exaggerated, then friends and acquaintances can be alienated. Or, one may play upon the sympathy of others to the degree of not undertaking tasks that could, and should, be undertaken alone. At the other extreme, a person may develop such an aversion to assistance that help is not asked for when a situation may involve the risk of complicating the original problem or aborting needed future growth. (Sometimes we need to be honestly assertive; other times we should be graciously dependent.)

There are two routes one can take in avoiding these extremes. One is the acceptance of one's condition, which was discussed earlier. In effect, a person must prevent his own egocentricity from getting in the way of self-understanding. The other aid to objectivity is to be sensitive to the advices and suggestions of relatives, friends, and professional helpers who have the capacity for "tough love."

There are many sources of potential help — private institutions, public funding, health and welfare agencies, and voluntary agencies. If necessary, relatives and friends can assist by researching what is available by contacting knowledgeable professionals in the local area or by simply spending some time in a local library.

To Summarize

Whenever you are confronted with an opportunity to make a new beginning after a life crisis, focus immediately upon HOW to use the experience. This is the creative response. When the approach is used, creative events begin to occur frequently. No one can anticipate the ways in which good news emerges from the so-called bad news when people focus upon how to use the totality of their experiences.

CHAPTER 7
IF YOU CAN'T SOLVE IT, COMPLICATE IT

The young tend to believe there is a solution to every problem; the old know there are some problems which cannot be solved. Between these two extremes, practical experience helps to determine the boundaries of possibility for each individual. Unfortunately, many people unnecessarily limit fulfillment of their hopes.

Often we limit ourselves by failing to reexamine our own assumptions. Or, we may simply be caught upon the hook of our inner fears. For example, we can do this by

- deciding prematurely that we do not have, or cannot acquire, the resources for the task ahead,
- giving up our efforts to solve a problem, after trying and failing with conventional solutions, or
- fearing future success, if our efforts should accomplish the goals.

It is always sad when a person's potential is artificially limited by one of these inner decisions. There are so many limiting factors in the universe over which we have no control whatsoever. So, when one of us adds such an unnecessary individual handicap to his or her burden, we grieve for that person.

For instance, I recall two student friends I had during my early twenties. Both of these individuals, one a woman and the other a man, were recognized as brilliant students with great promise. I can remember envying their ability to write beautiful, expressive English prose. They were the kind of students one finds on staffs of college annuals or newspapers. They could be expected regularly to whip out term papers and themes easily. Invariably, their papers received "A" or "A + " grades.

Through occasional alumni contacts, it has surprised me during the years since graduation that neither of these individuals has produced significant work for publication. Both of them have apparently never really tried for that goal. The years seem to have brought both of them a touch of pathetic bitterness.

Of course, the self-discipline, perseverance, and motivation which are required to do well in any field can be eroded by many self-defeating forces. So, it is suggested here that before you decide a problem cannot be overcome, you consider using a different approach to it.

If you have not been able to solve a problem through customary methods, try complicating it in one of the following ways:

1. Develop an innovative solution adapted to fit the special problem.
2. Find a second related problem and combine the two in a way that might yield a single solution for both of them.
3. Involve the ideas and self-interest of a few individuals who have strong motivation to solve one of the problems.

These approaches can be used in a wide variety of situations. A few illustrations are the self-help financing of college educations, building and financing a home residence on a limited income, promoting a needed change in city or county government, instituting a needed human relations program within a private industry, or program development within voluntary community organizations.

In the naïveté of youth, I used to assume that if anyone was confronted with a serious problem, he would respond positively to an original solution when it was suggested. Unfortunately, an experience during the World War II years disillusioned me of this assumption.

In the fall of 1943, along with other married couples coming to the University of Chicago campus for graduate studies, my wife and I shared in the problem of locating inexpensive, furnished apartments. We needed affordable space for ourselves and our five-year-old son. So, I took two days off work in Columbus, Ohio, and came to Chicago in July to look for a place available in late August.

The first day I went through all of the usual routes — the University Housing Office, classified ads, university bulletin board listings — with zero results. I could ill-afford to be away from work more than the allotted two days. So, it was necessary that a place be found the next day. The central problem was that with housing in such short supply, every vacancy was immediately filled by word of mouth prior to the time that the apartment managers needed to advertise it. As a stranger to the community, I had to find a way to access that process.

Returning to my hotel room, I tried to relax and concentrate upon putting everything I had learned during the day into my unconscious mind just before sleep. After a normal night's rest, I awoke the next morning with an idea which seemed workable.

The method was innovative, simple, and inexpensive. I outlined in red on a Chicago street map the residential area within a half mile of the campus boundary. With the map as a guide, I turned to the Yellow Pages listing of apartments on the south side of Chicago and wrote on a sheet of paper the addresses and telephone numbers for every apartment building within the red boundaries. Then, I called every apartment manager on the list to inquire about vacancies expected about the time we needed to move, apartment size, and furnishings and rental prices. I found nine places that seemed suitable.

Finally, I got into the car, visited each of these nine locations, interviewed the managers, and inspected the type of apartments which would be available. By elimination, I selected the best deal among the nine choices, went back immediately and paid a month's rent in advance. The entire task was complete before noon!

Since our rental worked out to an arrival date about a week before the fall term started, there were opportunities to meet other married couples arriving at the university with the same problem. They soon became desperate in their search for furnished apartments within their means. I was glad to share my alternative search method with twenty of these couples.

To my amazement, not one of these couples tried the plan. Instead, they all seemed to prefer the frustration of living temporarily with relatives, camping out with friends, paying exhorbitant rents or living in low-cost but relatively unaffordable motel rooms until they could locate apartments through the usual channels.

This kind of puzzling human action raises questions about our complex motivations. It has also aroused the curiosity of behavioral scientists. The comparison between the way we respond and the way other animals think is not always flattering.

For instance, from laboratory experiments with rats we know that if they are given a choice of four tunnels, where at the far end of the third there is a piece of cheese, they will explore them all, find the cheese, and eat it. Then, when cheese is placed, instead, at the end of tunnel number four, they will look for it in tunnel three. Finding nothing there, they will search through the others until the cheese is located and eat it.

Humans, presented with a similar type of problem, will often sit down at the equivalent of tunnel number three and complain that no food is available. Perhaps this has something to do with the fact that we possess complex memory linkages about ways that have been used to solve problems in the past. We may tend to be less orientated to one-day-at-a-time solutions of a problem than are more instinctive creatures. What are other possible reasons why we tend to resist original solutions?

The Fear of Being Thought Peculiar

There are many peer-group ideas among us about what is accepted as proper. Sometimes we impose handicaps upon ourselves by confusing normal human behavior with what is thought to be peculiar or a trifle crazy. We are afraid that if we deviate from the usual or customary methods in solving a problem, we will be considered odd.

If a problem is truly important in one's life and there is *any* feasible way it can be resolved, then one should try to overcome the difficulty in a way that meets one's ethical standards. The priority should not be placed upon whether someone in the community thinks the solution is peculiar or not.

The Fear of Success

We sometimes discard the option of approaches that might lead to success because we sense our experience in dealing with success is much more limited than our past familiarity with failure.

Also, in our society we have a tendency to worship the idol of the deadly average. Superiority or excellence at anything has come to be identified in many minds with being inhuman or being the kind of person with whom it is uncomfortable to associate.

Unconsciously, other individuals develop what has been called "success avoidance patterns." This is a very subtle but persistent kind of behavior. People having the pattern will appear to strive hard toward achieving success. Yet, always when it is almost within their grasp, they will do something that effectively aborts the final achievement.

Because of an unconscious fear of the risks of success, they avoid the rewards of innovative solutions to their problems. Creative problem solving is often stimulated by introducing what might seem, at first, to be a complicating factor of time delay.

The Time Element

It is easy to overlook or neglect to use fully the element of timing. Having constructed a neat solution to a problem, we sometimes find it cannot be applied. In other cases, when we apply our solution, it simply does not produce the desired results. Actually, the problem can be a simple one and yet entangle us in a complex net of frustration.

For instance, the owner of a small business discovered that occasionally after arriving at the office with a schedule in mind, or on paper, nothing seemed to be working in a synchronized way. He would start trying to make telephone calls, continuing or initiating small tasks. But people were not available that morning to answer the phone, expected individuals had left messages saying they would have to come on a later date, and his own deskwork was thrown out of the sequence needed for the day's objectives.

The timing for everything seemed off cycle. Then, it occurred to him that perhaps he was on the wrong cycle.

On mornings when that happened, he found an original approach that usually worked well. His house was about fifteen minutes round trip from the office. So, he would drive home, fix a cup of coffee there, pretend it was just the start of the day, and drive back to the office. He said that invariably, he would then have a new focus on the day — TIMING was different. People who could not previously be reached by phone, would be available, events would start to fall into sequence. He would have a satisfying, productive day.

Timing and the concerns of other people are vital in most kinds of activity. One of these is community group development.

A young pastor, who specialized in serving small-town churches, used a novel approach to group formation, such as youth groups, young adults, women's associations, and men's groups. When he first came to a new pastorate, the church would have the usual assortment of such organizations, but one or more would be semidormant and lacking in the depth of volunteer support needed for group vitality. Early on, he would quietly let the lame organization dwindle and finally find some excuse for announcing it would not meet anymore. If there was a genuine need for the group's activities, and there usually was, the demand for its resumption would begin to surface within a few months. When the requests reached the point where folks were beginning to *clamor* that the pastor *do* something, he would call a few of them together for a meeting.

"All right, I will provide staff assistance," he would tell them, "but it will be your group to plan and *support.*"

The timing would be right, because people were ready to become involved. The group would become vital and would grow.

In a more formal way, and on a larger scale, the same principle applies at the national level. During the early years of the Franklin D. Roosevelt presidency, one of Harry Hopkins' bright, young men was William J. Plunkert. He was assigned to various social organizations across the nation in connection with the New Deal programs.

During the later years of his career, in the 1950s and 1960s, Bill Plunkert held a position in New York City as national field director for a volunteer public health agency. From the wealth of his experience at both the local and national levels, Bill possessed a broad knowledge of community organization. One of the principles which he constantly shared was that of TIMING. Whenever one of the field persons in his department was considering the formation of an affiliate or chapter in a city, Bill took special pains to brief the staff member before every field trip and to debrief afterwards.

He would advise at every point that one should be sensitive to the timing. Did local people appear to be truly interested and committed at this time to the formation of an affiliate? Did they seem open to the suggestion that they ought to have representation from all major segments of the community in their planning? Was the climate of public opinion and past history of the community such that interest could be aroused for the affiliate's health objectives? Would the group be open to the suggestions of powerful people in the community who could provide access to adequate volunteer giving?

If there were too many negatives in response to such questions, Bill Plunkert would suggest that the project should be put on the back burner for six months or a year. Whether that was the decision or not, he would always emphasize that it was vital for staff to include in their plans a specific strategy for the next field visit to a city.

He continually emphasized, "If the timing is wrong, no amount of staff time or effort or travel expense will make up for that lack."

Urgency of Related Problems

As a young man, I read somewhere, "Grasp opportunity by the forelock; it is bald behind," meaning that one always needs to act quickly when opportunities present themselves.

For several years this seemed to be very wise advice. Until, that is, it became apparent that 1) many opportunities repeat themselves and 2) some of the better ones come when one has deliberately set up an environment favorable to their occurrence.

Situations sometimes develop in a way that all the essential factors are present. In addition to timing, the elements of such *complicating* opportunities include

1. the urgency of several problems,
2. one or more persistent, dedicated persons, and

3. the needed skills of a small group of concerned people.

Perhaps no group of people has displayed greater skill at doing what is often thought to be impossible than individuals of the Quaker Fellowship, especially when working through their American Friends' Service Committee. As background for our concerns it is helpful to know that the A.F.S.C. has undertaken projects throughout the world, wherever they have been able to obtain access. Within the range of their personnel and financial resources, they have tried to assist people to help themselves, whether the needs are acute problems of hunger, housing, health, education, or any of these as related to the effects of war.

The Committee has one objective: *to demonstrate love.*

The members and staff are reluctant to talk about that. While involved in a project, if they are really pushed to explain, "But why *are you* doing this for us?" they will try to state the objective simply. And then drop the subject.

They know that people in deep need have usually learned to be suspicious of strangers who arrive with assistance, particularly if they utter pious phrases or seem to have access to resources the needy folk do not understand. The A.F.S.C. people want nothing in return: no reimbursement, no subservience, not even recruitment to the Quaker fellowship. The result is a way of getting into "impossible situations" with some ideas for workable self-help solutions. To illustrate these methods, it will be useful to describe one A.F.S.C. project begun and completed during the 1950s decade.

This was an endeavor to demonstrate how self-help might be used to develop improved housing and living conditions in a slum area of Philadelphia. All of the usual problems and potential conflicts were present: absentee landlords and run-down, overcrowded rental housing, lack of financing, lack of indigent skills, interracial tensions, labor-management distrust, little prior experience with property ownership on the part of residents, and deep hopelessness about any possibility of change for the better.

As background, during the 1940s the Committee had undertaken two significant self-help housing projects that were successfully completed. The first was called Penn Craft in Fayette County, Pennsylvania, involving construction of 50 homes built by and for coal-mining families. Using the same pattern, a second project was undertaken in Lorain, Ohio. It completed 37 homes.

After the Penn Craft project was under way, a man by the name of A. Hurford Crosman had been put on the local Self-Help Committee staff. His assignment was to describe and promote the use of this approach so that other locations in the country might be able to consider using it.

Following the Fayette County and Lorain demonstrations of the approach, it was felt that a more difficult type of situation might be explored. Mr. Crosman was asked to take the assignment of investigating the possibilities in Philadelphia of doing a project in a slum area. If that seemed feasible, he was to proceed.

His first step was to get in touch with Bedford Settlement House to inquire whether they might be interested in being involved. They felt that a slum rebuilding project was outside their range. He then contacted another settlement house, The Friends' Neighborhood Guild, a Quaker organization. The response was strongly in favor of cooperation.

Next, he contacted officials at the Philadelphia City Hall. He described what the Self-Help Committees had done with housing at other locations and sketched how these methods could be applied to slum housing of the inner city. He then inquired, "Do you have any ideas about how we might get possession of an entire city block?"

Here he encountered the first set of *related problems,* which were to be immensely *helpful* as they were combined with the objectives of the A.F.S.C. The city had been deeply concerned about both the human conditions in the slum areas and the deteriorated buildings of the inner city. However, the problem at city hall was that the issues seemed so complicated the officials were pleased to find a knowledgeable group which had experience in demonstrating a solution.

They responded that they could give assistance: first, by helping to select an appropriate city block for such a project and, second, by getting possession of the property through the procedure of eminent domain. The procedure would enable them to obtain appraisals and offer a reasonable price to the present owners of the properties. Then, if the A.F.S.C. could find a means for financing the project, the subsequent cooperative organization would have the property at a feasible cost.

The area that was later selected was a block of three-story buildings, generally dating from the Civil War period, cut up into apartments and rented under the usual squalid conditions. Because of its location the program subsequently became known as the Eighth and Brown Streets Project.

The Eighth and Brown Streets Project

Next, William A. Clarke, chairman of the Self-Help Committee, and president of the National Mortgage Bankers Association, put Mr. Crosman in touch with the people at the local F.H.A. office.

Crosman presented the proposal, including the idea of renovating a whole block with the aid of people who would meet their *down payment* on a cooperative apartment *through self-help labor* on the project. The plan called for each family to make cash monthly payments to cover mortgage payments of a housing cooperative. After he had laid the projected plan out for review, the F.H.A. people responded by flatly turning the idea down. They did not like any of the main features, including the cooperative ownership idea, possible interracial complications, the self-help down payment plan, the slum location, or what they presumed to be Quaker naïveté.

How was the Committee to get around this major obstacle?

Here is one of the points at which the importance of getting influential people involved from various fields is illustrated. Mr. Clarke took Mr. Crosman to Washington, D.C., to see the national head of the Federal Housing Authority in the hope that more imagination might be encountered at that level. Again, they presented the whole package of what the Committee proposed to do. While still in his office, the F.H.A. executive called the Philadelphia office to instruct them to go ahead. The commitment of F.H.A. would be one million dollars to the project.

Returning home with the F.H.A. commitment, the Committee was able to get approval for a loan from the Philadelphia Savings Fund Society in the amount of $500,000 to complete the first half of the project.

Meanwhile, during the time that these events were taking place, the Friends' Neighborhood Guild had been sponsoring a series of meetings among local people to explain the objectives of the Committee. The Guild had the confidence of the community and this enabled Crosman to participate in these contacts. People who attended the meetings were informed that the A.F.S.C. had put in about $100,000 of its own contributed money toward the project. And it was explained the A.F.S.C. had done this, not to make money, but to start some action that would show what could be done through self-help.

The meetings were aimed at three principle objectives:
1. to explain and discuss the general purposes of the plan,
2. to defuse any interracial conflicts, and
3. to obtain labor cooperation, particularly in view of the fact that purchasers of apartments would be contributing labor toward the cost.

Excellent results were obtained on all these objectives. The people at the Guild were thoroughly familiar with the Quaker method of gaining consensus through open discussion of issues. In this approach, great patience is exercised in holding as many meetings as necessary and following up with other related groups, as needed. The moderators are skilled in persistently staying with the "sense of the meeting" until some rational next step can be agreed upon, leaving people amicably communicating with one another. Not until these community hurdles were surmounted did the actual procedure of eminent domain begin.

The Committee engaged an architect who redesigned the entire block into 88 modern apartments with an open courtyard in the center. The Friends' Neighborhood Guild had been chosen to have charge of selecting people who would be given opportunities to buy cooperative apartments.

Finally, a Quaker building contractor, a Mr. Unkefer, was given the contract for the project, with the understanding that he would be responsible for providing new owners with guidance in doing and/or learning jobs — painting, carpentry, etc. For instance, a single woman learned to lay tile for her bathroom floor. She became so good at this that she got the job of laying 88 bathroom floors!

After the project was half finished, it was necessary for Mr. Crosman to find a bank to furnish the other half-million dollars of financing. Starting at the obvious spot, the largest Quaker bank, the Provident Trust Company, he got a flat "No."

So, he next went to the Fidelity Philadelphia Trust Company and asked the vice president in charge of real estate loans to come with him to see what they had done at the project. The vice president responded by inviting Mr. Crosman to a luncheon, where he was given an opportunity to tell the story to all the vice presidents of the firm. After that presentation, he was told "Mr. Crosman, please leave the room."

Soon he was asked back and told they would finance the loan for $500,000.

After returning to his office. Crosman's phone rang. It was the executive in charge of real estate loans. In telling about the incident afterwards, Mr. Crosman recalled, "I felt my heart would stop."

"You told us," the voice continued, "that F.H.A. would only allow us to charge 4 1/2% interest. We've decided we'll grant the loan at 4% because we wish to have a small say in what you are doing to help rebuild the slums of Philadelphia." (On a forty year mortgage 1/2% interest amounted to a sizable gift.)

The whole project was finally completed in something less than a decade of effort. Almost 30 years afterwards, Hurford Crosman had an opportunity to revisit the site in Philadelphia. I quote from his comments after he returned from that trip:

> The court in the middle of the buildings, which they had cleaned of trash and planted to trees and lawns, is today even more beautiful than when I left the place.

> I learned that during the ensuing years neither bank has ever missed a monthly payment. So, the cooperative ownership, which many people said would never work, has worked.[1]

In a brief, capsule description, the above example shows how COMPLEXITIES can be pulled together so that IMPOSSIBLE problems of many people can be solved. All the essential elements were brought into this mixture: timing, several difficult problems, a dedicated person with coordination skills, and a core group of concerned people.

If you can't solve it, try complicating it!

CHAPTER 8
IF I SHOULD DIE BEFORE I WAKE

Many parents in this country used to teach their children a bedtime prayer, which was sometimes phrased in these words:

Now I lay me down to sleep.
I pray the Lord my soul to keep.
If I should die before I wake,
I pray the Lord my soul to take.

For some imaginative children the nightly repetition of this prayer produced two opposite reactions.

The reference to dying in one's sleep tended to heighten imaginary fears. Shadows in a dark corner of a bedroom or a hallway assumed ominous shapes. The darkness outside of the window could hold other imaginary terrors. At times, a child could become quite fearful that death might occur at any moment.

On the other hand, once the prayer had been said, it might take on a kind of magical influence. With a good-night kiss from a parent, one could snuggle into the bed-covers with a feeling that whatever unknown fears might lurk in the night, a shield of protection had been pulled down around the place of sleep.

As we grow into adulthood, there usually comes an awareness that it is not the threat of mortal extinction itself which seems to terrify us. Instead, it is the contrast between the creative abilities we may possess and the fragile mortality in which these accumulated talents and skills are housed.

We dread the threat of a life cut short before we have had time to accomplish something significant. Or, as popularly expressed today, time to make a statement which has meaning for us. For many people, especially those who were born after the midpoint of this century, the risk of atomic annihilation carries a threat that achievement may be prematurely cut off.

Since August 1945 we have lived with The Bomb. At first there were a few people who sensed the great changes that nuclear energy would bring. Some of us wrote prophetic, but slightly hysterical, articles about the new atomic age.[1,2] We could not anticipate the positive effects of atomic energy. One of these was the military nuclear deterrent, which made it necessary for great powers to avoid another world war. We were able at least to be free of that horror to the time of the present writing — for 41 years after Hiroshima.

Gradually, more and more people became aware of the issues, including controversial information about the disposal of atomic waste material. Also, after the accumulation of weapons stockpiles, primarily by the U.S.A. and the U.S.S.R., it became known that there were thousands of atomic warheads and hundreds of bomb delivery machines.

Thus, as the balance of deterrence became more costly and precarious, increasing numbers of people also felt acutely apprehensive about risks and uncertainties connected with all aspects of nuclear energy and its control. Two generations of humankind have been born and reached adulthood since 1945. In the industrial countries these individuals have done much of their growing up during a period when a scornful attitude has prevailed toward the lessons of history and past philosophical thought. This means that large numbers of people know the feeling of terror about death, but have had less inner equipment to deal with that than some of those who had reached adulthood prior to the atomic age.

People in older generations need somehow to find more ways of sharing their understandings with the younger ones. We all need to tap into the best resources of our experiences with faith. More of us need to rediscover that our terror of death is one of the principal things which motivate our lives, our choices, our accomplishments, and the whole structure of relationships.[3] Soren Kierkegaard, the illustrious Danish philosopher and theologian, had brilliantly explored this theme. He understood humankind's effort to avoid facing the "terror, perdition (and) annihilation (that) dwell next door to every man."[4]

But in facing that reality, younger people need to know that among the older generations there were individuals who had found an understanding of life's meaning and an acceptance of death. I can only speak now from my own experience in seeking serenity in today's world.

It helps any of us a great deal if during childhood or youth we have an opportunity to become acquainted with serene, aging persons in the home environment. We frequently see newspaper articles mentioning that many children and teenagers are now growing up without frequent exposure to grandparents.

As a small boy, I had an opportunity to see one of my grandmothers in residence in my parents' home for several years. Aside from the fact that this gave me a greater appreciation for family history and continuity, I also learned to know grandmother *as a person*.

In her childhood, the family home in southern Wisconsin was in pioneer territory. She told me of watching Native Americans go through the woods along a trail that was visible from the log cabin her father had built. As she told about many of her recollections from those years, I came to feel that a bridge of understanding had been built between us.

I began to see her, not as a wrinkled, old woman with a cane and some difficulty in walking, but someone with whom I could communicate. We could ask each other questions. We could share some of our thoughts. She had the time to talk with a small boy, who was exploring his own world and had a need for her love. As her physical energies decreased still further, we observed her moving into feebleness. Then, she declined into a period of several weeks of being bedfast with what became her fatal illness.

This sturdy, gentle woman, born on Christmas Day of 1843, who had married at age 24, given birth to ten children, seen seven of them raised to adulthood, finally died at age 80. She went away from us as she had lived — gently and sturdily with a combination of acceptance and affirmation.

To a boy of eleven years, this was a mysterious event, but not in any way frightening. I saw death as a normal part of life.

In contrast, one can observe in some children between the ages of eight and twelve a tendency to view older people as strange, freakish creatures, who easily become the butt for cruel and vandalizing pranks. One wonders how much less difficult the adjustment to aging, mortality and death might be for such children when they reach adulthood, if they had personal opportunities to know older people as companions and friends.

And here it is obvious that each of us can begin to do something about the problem, if we have not already done so. One of the more positive occurrences within many retirement communities are the organized efforts of churches and schools to develop activities that bring school children, junior high, and high school youths together with older populations. The beneficial results from such programs can be seen almost immediately in the changed attitudes toward modern youth on the part of older persons and in the increased appreciation and friendship with older individuals that develop among younger people. There is something that shatters the false images and stereotypes when a youth encounters a person who smiles and without hesitation says, "I just turned 74," or "I will be 91 next birthday." It does not take very much more conversation for a younger person to sense that this is an individual who has done a good job of coming to terms with his or her mortality.

And for the older person who may have gotten somewhat out of touch, a mental image of today's youth as predominantly thoughtless or delinquent also needs revision.

The personal benefits, when one is young, of forming some friendships with older people is something everyone can experience. We focus more specifically upon those benefits in the chapter entitled "What Zestful Oldsters Can Teach Us." The habit is one that each individual should cultivate. Getting acquainted with older people is very easy. For a start, if they are retired and still living in their own homes, they can usually use a little help from strong younger arms and legs to run some errands or fix something around the yard. If a younger adult simply sets aside a couple of hours a week to be helpful in the neighborhood, he or she will find one or two alert, interesting oldsters with whom to become a friend.

Once you get accustomed to forming some friendships outside your own age group, the habit is apt to persist. So, if one finally grows old, the habit turns around the other direction. It then becomes easy to make friends among younger persons. This is part of joining the human family. And the habit of always joining is one which, in itself, helps to keep off the "excess fat" of egocentricity.

Death becomes a terror to us when egocentricity grows unchecked. Always, as we seek to save ourselves for ourselves, we save nothing, but become increasingly alone — and more terrified in our aloneness.

In contrast, when egocentricity is surrendered and we feel most a part of the human race, we become increasingly comfortable in our private aloneness. We learn to enjoy the quietness of our personal inner spaces as a daily experience. As we become truly acquainted with ourselves, we are able with more security to reach out to others and to be more open when others reach out to us. We begin to feel that we are more a part of our universe.

Eventually, when we sense the nearness of death, there seems to come an experience of being in familiar company, even though at this point each person stands alone.

Acceptance of One's Mortality

A precondition for creative coping with death is acceptance of one's personal status as mortal. For some, the acceptance may occur rather traumatically shortly before death. But is is far better, and a more normal growth process, if an individual gets into that acceptance at an earlier age.

There is a similarity between accepting the reality of death and accepting the fact of any other crisis. People who overcome major crises in their younger years have often commented how fortunate they later felt that the experience came early enough to enjoy their recoveries.

One of the great disabling and handicapping myths in our culture is based upon the illusion, "I shall expect and plan as though I will always remain as mobile, as healthy, and as independent as I am today." We often seem to act as though we thought there was some virtue, some indication of strength, in promoting the image of ourselves as exceptions to the rule of mortal decay, decline, and fallibility. We go whistling through life with all the bravado of small children walking through a village cemetery; whereas, the only people truly capable of walking casually by the symbols of death are those who have totally accepted the fact that one day their physical remains will join the company of those symbols.

As we move into the middle years, we acquire large investments in our personal knowledge and skills. The years and the training, the education and the earlier work experience, have gotten us to a point where we can, perhaps, make a contribution to our families and to society. We become increasingly aware that the sum of our knowledge, usually very hard-earned, is precariously housed within fragile tissues. Illnesses, accidents, or calamity could easily wipe out all that we have to give, not to mention the personal joy of having time to practice our skills and arts.

This focus of concern, and perhaps some anxiety, about one's mortality is the usual pattern for thoughtful, mature people. But the person who has begun to form the habit of NOW-living soon discovers a new and entirely different focus regarding the reality and meaning of life.

NOW-Living Shifts One Sideways

Yet, many of one's actions and choices appear to continue in paths previously followed. For instance, a person usually continues to strive toward goals and the achievement of short-term objectives. In fact, you would probably discover that you are now organizing your efforts better, carrying them out with less anxiety, and, thus, actually able to concentrate more energy upon your selected schedules of the day than you did previously.

The only change in your behavior that may be observable to other people may be in the consistency and thoroughness with which you attend to good preventative maintenance standards for your own body. Perhaps a reason for that is you have so totally accepted the fragility of the mortal body that you now give extra effort to prevent it from falling apart any sooner than necessary.

Another reason could be the sense of relaxation and enjoyment that seems to characterize people living in the NOW. These individuals are not obsessive about their own bodies — either their wellness or their potential ailments. But they are apt to follow appropriate regimens of diet, exercise, recreation, work, and meditation. Attention is given to a balance of all five of these activities into a combination that seems best suited to the individual's self-knowledge. Individuals who have occasion to learn about such a person's diet, work, or exercise regimen are often inclined to comment, "You must have a lot of willpower to stick with that."

However, willpower does not seem to describe the personal experience of people who live in this manner. They are merely doing what seems natural and comfortable to them. From the perspective of others, the schedule appears difficult, rigorous, or disagreeable. But from the *NOW-perspective,* the person's life is in the style requiring *the least effort.*

The big changes are in the person's inner sense of focus — a different way of perceiving

1. the ultimate meaning of one's life,
2. how we evaluate what we do, and
3. the way death is confronted.

The Creative Universe

Whenever we become willing to turn our lives over to a Power greater than ourselves, we open the door to acceptance of the reality that we do not know and cannot truly control the ultimate value of anything we do. And, when we can thoroughly accept that only God is ultimately in charge of what life is for, the terror of death will also begin to lose its power.

That acceptance will bring about some marked personality changes. These will be most noticeable on the part of the individuals who previously had tended to be very controlling, both of their own lives and of their closest associates. Individuals who had previously been obsessive, long-range life planners will have a struggle in trying to adapt to the new concept. In a sense, they had always tried to play God with their own lives and/or the lives of other people, when they could. If they discover that this behavior is not suitable, necessarily effective, or appropriate to the role of humankind, the shock can be heavy. The difficulty will be that they are not in the habit of trusting anyone, much less God, with anything as important as their own lives.

Perspective Upon Life Meaning

Acceptance that God has charge of the ultimate results and purpose of life will affect one's attitudes about aging, the threat of physical infirmities, the fragility of mortal tissue and premature interruptions of careers.

If you had been living under the older concepts to any degree, the usual cultural standards about accomplishments and public recognition of your efforts were important. At the very least, you had become attached to your notions about what it meant to fulfill oneself through the bearing and raising of children, preparing yourself for some line of work, and performing some recognizably useful service with it. Perhaps you had dreamed of creating a new art form or inventing some new and useful equipment.

Each individual develops a set of dreams and aspirations. These may appear to be foolish to other people, but they are important to the individual. The difficulty occurs when we begin to attach too much life-significance to these particular dreams. Then, as a younger person, if you become fearful that under the threat of global catastrophe you will not live long enough to achieve these objectives, a deep pessimism can become the underlying tone of your feelings.

But now, let us assume you have discovered a new perspective through a commitment of your life. From your present view, the so-called success standards and leaving one's mark in life have become nonessential. If you go the next step beyond that liberating idea, you become open to the mind-expanding horizon of a universe which has a much larger and more meaningful plan than the prior earthbound provincialisms. Even if your individual place in that pattern is microscopic in proportion to the plan's immensity, there is no problem for you. Knowing the place or time where your slot may fit into the whole is no longer an important issue to you. You are *now* part of whatever the universe is about in its business. You belong there. You belong here.

You trust the loving Power to which you have committed your life, and you have decided to live one day at a time in that trust. You have discovered that prior efforts at trying to be the Big I — trying to play God — in ultimate control of your life did not work in a manageable way. So, the NOW will be enough for your focus. However, you will be attempting to do things the easy way — the "in line with the grain of the universe" way.

How do we get satisfaction in our daily lives when we do not know the ultimate purpose of the processes in which we are engaged? That question only appears complicated to the person who has not yet taken the step of making the commitment of turning his life over to the Power greater than self. After one has made the choice and gotten a bit comfortable in the new state of affairs, the answer to the question becomes simple and direct.

You get your satisfaction from functioning — from the process, not from knowing its end result. There are everyday things which you enjoy doing and unexpected things which stimulate interest. Some of the unscheduled things add to the intrigue of new problems to solve. Others bring rewards of small satisfactions. If you are active in pursuits that are within the range of your skills — things you enjoy doing — there will seldom be days of boredom.

Evaluating What We Do

Yet, within that focus of ultimate meaning we need a measurement for our personal day-by-day efforts. The goal is to do one's best. But what is "our best" in NOW terms? It is certainly not superiority to others. Rather, the measurement is against the yardstick of one's yesterday. In one sense, there is no such thing as the best performance. This is not an absolute term. It is actually only a concept that gets its meaning in comparison with something else. So, within our present focus and on the short term, we refer merely to the fact that some of the time we seem to be improving, while on other occasions we are getting worse. We are making steady efforts to improve.

In measuring improvement against one's yesterday, there always has to be the relaxed awareness that some mistakes will be made and some lessons are there to be learned. This is part of the fun that awaits us in every new day, provided we approach it with a sense of humor about ourselves.

In looking backward, usually one is quite amazed to discover how persistent is the tendency to make the same, tired old mistakes over and over. After a while, we usually learn to accept that fact and be more tolerant of ourselves. We are all creatures of habit. For example, people in their middle years tend to discontinue the practice of making New Year's resolutions. They discover that real change takes a different and deeper approach than mere willpower.

When you make a comparison between what you did yesterday and what you are doing today, care should be taken that your attention is directed at the lesson you think yesterday provided. Otherwise, it is always easy to slip back into the older pattern of either feeling guilty about something we did or its related game of "what if I had done this or that?" These games, and the false guilt which often accompanies them, should be avoided.

A proper attitude is to say to oneself, "Okay, I did such-and-such a thing yesterday. It did not work out too well. But it seemed like a good decision at the time. Now that I have learned what seems to be a better approach, I will try to benefit from that lesson in every today."

Even after a fairly short time of living with commitment to a Higher Power and a focus upon one-day- or one-now-at-a-time efforts, the shift will noticeably change one's attitude toward death. As time passes the alteration becomes more permanent.

The Way Death Is Confronted

First, one moves immediately into the acceptance stage of feelings, since that is where one has been living. Except, perhaps to check whether one is currently up to date, a person will have no need to go through any of the prior, classic stages that have been described in the literature as characteristic of the terminally ill.

If you are following this lifestyle, and you have temporarily slipped a little from that pattern, you will be able to get back to it very quickly. Sometimes in the speed of events, or the preoccupation with urgent demands upon your energy, you may drift away from the immediacy of inner consciousness. Or, you may have temporarily neglected quiet times of meditation. But you will have formed the habit of checking your navigation points periodically. It is not really comfortable sailing without knowing your position, even in a calm sea.

If you have been on this track for any length of time, you have frequently discovered it was necessary to make small course corrections when old habit patterns begin to divert your route. Another good comparison is with the practices of health maintenance. Once a person is accustomed to a healthy regimen of diet and exercise, any diversionary push which starts to derail the pattern can be quickly picked up and corrected. Most of the time, one becomes unaware of such minor deflections in any regular routine — whether it is steering a boat, the maintenance of health, or now-living.

Another characteristic of persons focused upon the present is their quiet inner sense of peace and vibrancy. These feelings generally run intermingled constantly within the consciousness. It is not a mere sense of acceptance or compensation for the terror of death. It is another kind of perception altogether — an inner affirmation that death has no terror. The evidence is perhaps best seen in the fact that when one of these individuals is notified of terminal illness by a physician, the classic stages of adjustment are bypassed. With only the least delay, they move immediately into the acceptance stage.

Of course, there is no way one can prove in a scientific manner that the life-focus causes the serenity.

One can only observe and consider how people with different focus commitments cope with similar crises. Our society has such concern about the risks of nuclear deterrence of war that examples of coping are not hard to find.

One of the more sensitive, intelligent voices to analyze the issues recently is Lewis Thomas, a scientist with impeccable reputation and achievements. He also happens to be a humanist.

In a short essay[5] he discusses his response to the realization that nuclear war would destroy a major portion, at minimum, of the planet. All of the hopes and dreams, all of the unfinished discoveries of medicine, of human betterment, of bright young persons just beginning to explore the powers of their imagination and skills would probably be lost or set backward for uncounted decades or centuries.

Then, from his viewpoint as a scientist, this gentle, caring person tries to imagine himself in the role of a young adult today. He feels that he would indeed want to give up trying to explore anything or learn anything.

In contrast, there is a hopeful viewpoint of ultimate purpose, I think. At least for myself I have chosen the way of tough, informed, sensitive now-living.

CHAPTER 9
THE CARE AND MAINTENANCE
OF THE BRAIN

We know just enough of the human brain to be sure it is the greatest marvel of the physical universe. Every advance of our recent knowledge surprises us with the complexity of the brain and reveals further unexplored mysteries about its functions.

In an effort to make this bundle of nerve tissues within us more understandable, we have sometimes compared the brain to a very sophisticated computer system. Indeed, in many ways it does work like a computer. However, it is also more than that. If we think that this most important organ of the person is merely a mechanism, we seriously downgrade ourselves. For we need to remember that the brain is more complex and more versatile than its product — the computer system.

Computers do not yet repair or improve themselves! For instance, hardly a month goes by without the appearance of a news feature about someone whose brain overcame what seemed to be an insurmountable obstacle. The difficulty may have been caused by an injury or a birth defect. Yet, an apparent miracle of determination, spirit, caring, and mental adaptation had occurred.

Until recent years knowledge about the organ's activities was often inexact. Now, electronic measuring devices can be attached to the skull to study brain-wave patterns during waking and sleeping hours. Scientists are also becoming more familiar with the subtle chemical signals which

119

activate and suppress brain cell activities. The amazing chemical processes that are performed within these tissues are just beginning to be understood.

This most intimate of all our organs has remained unobserved and mysterious to most of us. The brain is not only housed in a place where we cannot see or touch it, other sensory input is denied us also. Its tissue does not beat like the heart nor rumble like the intestinal tract. So, most of the time we ignore the brain and hope that somehow it will continue to work properly.

Yet, we know today that twenty percent of one's blood and oxygen supply is needed to handle this little bundle of tissue — an organ which accounts for only about two percent of the body's total weight! In an adult that weight is about three pounds.[1]

Perhaps you thought that the big muscles of your body did the *heavy* work? If so, think again. Even if you consider yourself a nonintellectual (whatever that is), the heavy work load of keeping alive and functioning is carried by that strange, hidden organ located within a cage of bone above your shoulders.

Since our brains are not equipped to store calories or the oxygen to convert them to energy, interruption of the blood supply is dangerous. Unconsciousness will occur in only ten seconds, if blood flow is stopped. Another vital physical need is the maintenance of spinal fluid, which provides a water bed to cushion the brain against external shock. There must be a flow of vitamins, other chemical compounds, and mineral elements essential to nerve tissue health. In its return, the blood flow carries away the waste products, which would poison the cells, if not removed. Indeed, among all of our wonderfully and awesomely made bodily cells none deserve more respect than those which compose the several different kinds of brain tissue.

Aside from keeping emotionally, physically and spiritually fit, what do we need to *know* and *do* to assist in the

120

proper care and maintenance of the brain? There are three areas we shall discuss here:

1. Without a review of anatomy, how does the brain work?
2. How can we help in providing physical supplies and protection?
3. What can we do to improve the brain's quality of thought and level of service?

Operation and Coordination of Bodily Functions

As we learned in school health courses, there are two kinds of muscles: the involuntary, such as heartbeat, digestive processes, temperature control, or the manufacturing of chemical compounds; and the voluntary muscle actions, ranging all the way from those used in chewing our food, playing musical instruments, smiling, scowling, walking, or running. The brain controls both of these.

The other major bodily operation is that by which the brain receives information through the five senses of hearing, touching, smelling, seeing, and tasting. These are really borderline functions between voluntary, involuntary, and brain action itself. For instance, the nerve endings in the nasal passages which sense odors are actually brain tissue!

Considered in their sum, the bodily functions just listed are, in themselves, both complex and basic. Each involves particular segments and combinations of segments within the brain. We will not explore these complexities here. If you do wish to become familiar with them in more detail, there are some good books for the lay reader, which can now be gotten through public libraries.

Memory

Often, when this subject is mentioned in conversation, people start to talk about their ability, or lack of ability, to memorize facts — names, faces, dates, or trivia. That skill is indeed part of memory, but such data are only a small tip of the iceberg called "memory." Our heads contain vast quantities of learned experiences and information. Without the ability to store, organize under crossfiles of related topics, and TO RECALL needed information upon DEMAND we could not function as human beings. Within our memories are filed items ranging from how to tie shoelaces to being able to hear and translate into meanings the vocal sounds of spoken languages. Everything from the primary skill of walking upright to the appreciation of music is stored in our brains. *And each person's set of "memory banks" contain a unique impression of experience.* For instance, many individuals can associate personal events with the physical scars accumulated through the years.

The Scars of Experience

I have a deep scar across the middle of my left eyebrow. It is reminder of an auto accident many years ago, before the time when cars were equipped with seat belts. So violent was the impact that the *left* side of my face became the projectile which smashed the *right* rear window glass.

The memories associated with that experience are surely only partly similar to those of the other five occupants of the sedan. Perhaps for all of us there is still a recollection of the vivid sounds of squealing tires, shattering glass, and tearing car body metal. Other associations relate to the college junior-senior banquet, which was to have been our destination that evening. For me, the recollections are also connected with several personal events, which set this scar apart from any of the many other pieces of scar tissue on my body.

I am reminded of the car's driver, my friend and classmate, Cornie Thiessen, who later served for many terms as a member of the Montana State Legislature; of his bride-to-be, Ailee Buck, who sat in the middle of the front seat; of my bride-to-be, Alice Reinholdt, who occupied the right front spot, directly ahead of me; and also Cornie's brother,

John, who was on my left in the middle of the rear seat. A woman, whose name eludes me, was in the left rear seat — the only one who did not need to go to the hospital for at least a checkup.

Some personal events of the next few days are also vivid, two in particular. Aside from being vigorously shaken up, Alice had no injuries except for a small abrasion on the right temple. However, a couple of days later her whole face began to swell until both eyes were almost shut. The diagnosis was called "gangrene and tetanus gas poisoning." She was immediately admitted to the hospital and given a tetanus shot. By the following morning she had apparently passed a crisis but was kept a few days in the hospital for observation.

Perhaps these experiences convinced us that we did not wish to have a longer engagement and separate, even temporarily, to return to our respective homes 1,400 miles apart. Anyhow, we decided, while I was still hospitalized, that we would get married immediately after college graduation.

So much for the memories connected with one scar. In only the most sketchy way does this example illustrate how rich and varied are the individual memories which can be associated with a scar from one's experiences.

The Levels of Memory

There are two major memory levels: those readily recallable in the conscious mind, and the larger, but more inaccessible, body of impressions stored in what we call the unconscious mind.

The conscious memory only connects with a limited number of experiences at a time. (Occasionally, when we find an individual who can recall material from many hundreds of books read during past years, it is so unusual that we label such a person a "genius.")

The various recall levels of the unconscious memory record and process a much larger volume of data. This storage resource not only contains information in great detail, but also permanently records one's feelings: the hurts, the joys, humiliations, and laughter about oneself.

It is the combined recording of the conscious and unconscious memories, plus the manner in which individual brains process these recordings, which make up what we call personality.

We record the events of the day in our memories as they occur. At the time, we usually only assimilate or digest these events to the degree necessary to make what we think are appropriate responses. It is later, often during sleep, that more complex associations are made within deeper levels of the mind. Our immediate responses are largely determined by our accustomed *habit patterns*.

For instance, suppose a woman applies at a personnel office for a position in a company. After completing the application form, she takes it to the interviewer, who informs her, "I'm sorry, there has been a mistake. That position was filled last week, but I was not notified until just a few minutes ago."

The applicant's response will depend upon a variety of circumstances, such as past experiences, how desperate is her need for the job, her personal reaction to the personality and voice tone of the interviewer, or the degree to which she has learned to accept frustration. Her reaction may be less irritable if she has learned to identify with the embarrassment of another person who has made an error. The memory of this event at the personnel office will be filed in both the conscious and the unconscious levels of the mind, but within the latter a greater wealth of emotional experiences may lie in wait to attach themselves to the incident.

The depth and the time span of conscious memory retention will be determined by

1. how much emotional power infuses the incident, and
2. how often the incident will be usefully recalled and retold in later social contacts.

After our brains have filed events of the day in the unconscious mind levels, they must be digested or related to all of the previous information and feeling already stored in that memory system.

The Data Base for Thought

Our minds are not simply data banks. They record and act upon

1. information received from the senses and processed through mental logic, and also
2. the emotional coloration we feel toward those factual events.

In thinking about how we think, we often overlook the emotional factors. Each person likes to imagine himself to be entirely logical or reasonable in personal opinions. It is only *other people* who are illogical or prejudiced, especially whenever they do not agree with us.

During recent years, research into the functions of sleep and dream life have hinted at some important parts of our unconscious thought processes. During sleep our deeper mind levels play back "the tapes" of the previous day's memories and integrate these recollections with the larger body of previously recorded feelings and information. A small portion of the mental digestion process surfaces in the form of dreams after we awake from sleep.

Usually, it is only when new events are emotionally frightening that the dream images are recalled with strong anxiety. Anxiety feelings will seldom occur with minds which are quite well integrated and comfortable within themselves.

Maintenance of Brain Objectivity

A person who *understands and accepts* with humor what is happening within the mind process can give conscious direction and assistance to the unconscious mind. When disturbing dreams are recalled upon waking, assurance can be given to the unconscious mind by a reminder that the remnants of childhood anxieties or insecurities are acceptable. Or, one can review the recent events which may have triggered ego-threatening or self-pitying feelings. In so doing, the events are put into a framework of adult, present-moment understanding. The unconscious is being told, "Refile these events under adult understandings and delete them from the file of old childhood bumps and bruises."

If such simple home remedies of mental health do not easily and quickly relieve emotional pressure, then deeper, unresolved problems may be present which should be looked into through professional counseling. Whenever any one of us either has repeated experiences of anxiety dreams or a nearly total inability to recall dream images, it is probable that the power and objectivity of the mind could be greatly increased through the aid of some counseling and psychotherapy.

Until recently, there was a tendency among psychologists and others in the social studies to overemphasize the factors of environment, training, and social conditioning upon human behavior. Now, with new research into genetics, the behavior of identical twins and adopted twins, the pendulum has begun to swing in the opposite direction.

It is increasingly clear that each of us enters life with a genetic-chemical imprint within the brain's "computer hardware." This imprint sets a pattern for the manner in which the individual mind does its thinking. Even when two individuals reach the same conclusion, they may not have arrived at it through similar thought processes. Realization of such facts should help to make us reverent about the complexity of the brain's performance and tolerant of the individual differences among us.

Acquired Mental Programming

Each human being starts with whatever the genetic-chemical imprint may be. With only the exception of individuals who incur severe brain damage and deprivation,

126

mental potential is usually so great that most people can learn to function at levels high enough to surprise themselves. Only ten percent (about 100 billion) of the brain's cells are active at any given time. The remainder are apparently a reserve for purposes of
1. replacement as active cells die as we age, and
2. replacement when cells are impaired by temporary lack of nourishment and/or by injury.

Increasingly, case studies are appearing in medical literature of persons whose memory records and skills have been impaired by brain injuries. Yet, they have often been able to achieve remarkable results through relearning and retraining.

For those of us who have experienced serious crises and are given the opportunity to restructure our thinking, the potential is especially great. We have been provided with the motivation to reprogram some of our mental processes. Without such motivation, most people do not get jarred out of their customary ruts, even though old patterns may have proven to be ineffective ways of coping.

It is within the subtle, imaginative brain processes that humankind's greatest mental distinction lies. One does not need to become a recognized poet to live poetically; nor a famous artist to live artistically. The objective of the mind is not to receive acclaim as a saint, a statesman, or an accumulator of wealth. The objective is to live creatively with love.

Physical Brain Care

Providing the brain with proper nourishment should be included as a major objective of general health maintenance. Unfortunately, this is not usually part of our thinking. When one hears about the desirability of regular exercise, balanced diet or avoidance of elements poisonous to the body, the effects upon the brain are seldom mentioned. Yet, if we knock out a portion of the main switchboard, what good are healthy abdominal organs or body muscles? A diet relying too heavily upon alcohol for calories can cause nutritional diseases of the brain, since alcoholic beverages do not contain the vitamins or minerals the brain tissues must have. A fat-loaded food supply risks arterial fatty deposits which, in turn, can impair blood flow to the brain.

The brain continues its activity while we are asleep, since there are necessary functions it must perform during regular sleep periods. As we have noted, it is during sleep that the unconscious digestion of conscious events occurs. Studies show that if persons are artificially kept awake over long periods, the individual develops psychotic-like symptoms. This has long been known and used as a part of torture in so-called brainwashing.

So, the first concern of brain care is to care for one's general health: balanced diet, adequate rest, regular physical exercise, and avoidance of whatever may be a tissue poison for the individual. (For a person with diabetes, drug dependency, alcoholism, or inability to digest certain foods properly, a "poison" may be a substance which has little harm for individuals not afflicted with such ailments.)

A second element of physical brain care is to avoid, in so far as possible, blows to the head which may cause concussion or bone penetration. The protective membrane, spinal fluid, and cranial bones provide a sheath that is remarkably effective. However, there are obviously serious limits to what this system can withstand.

Normal Brain Cell Loss

Unlike most body cells, those in the brain do not replace themselves as the original cells die. The large reserve of inactive cells partially compensates for this decline, particularly when we continue to keep mentally active.

About the time we reach the age of 21, our brain cells are dying fast enough that approximately one gram of the organ's weight will be lost each year for the rest of our lives.[2] As we get past the half-century mark there will be measurable declines in some mental capacities, particularly in the speed with which we can solve logical problems. Those of us who had previously developed great skill in shifting total concentration rapidly from one problem to another during the working day will also discover that we cannot change focus as rapidly as we did when younger. We may still be able to concentrate about as well as we did during college age, but it takes more time to get all of our attention centered on a single problem. Part of our retained skill is probably the result of our long years of continued experience. If we have kept mentally active, we possess a level of wisdom not yet achieved by younger people.

Some of the sensory capacities will also slow down with age. Which ones will vary somewhat between individuals, but all senses are apt to be affected: hearing, taste, smell, vision and sensitivity of touch. Some loss of keenness in sense of balance can become a risk, since older bones are more brittle and falls when walking are more dangerous.

Programming Changes in the Older Years

After about age 60 we begin to lose some of our capacity to reprogram and to develop new mental program systems for ourselves. Probably these changes are caused by two factors. First, the brain now has fewer unused reserve cells to draw upon for reprogramming. Second, for reasons not yet entirely researched, the chemical-electrical circuitry cannot respond as well when we try to shift our concentration rapidly from one subject to another.

These results of aging slow down the mechanism for learning complex, new patterns, as well as the capacity for rapid recall from memory. Therefore, it becomes much more important that older persons previously have established systems of balanced, flexible, fulfilling habit patterns.

If such patterns have been well developed in the early and middle years, the special talent of older people — sensitivity to the spiritual aspects of life — can be exercised with great zest. Normally, their ability to concentrate mentally is not impaired. Unless brain disease is present, their abilities of mental concentration remain amazingly sharp. The brain is simply not a top producer of new programming systems nor of tasks which require rapid switching from one subject to another.

Especially in the late seventies and after age 80, another problem is sometimes misnamed loss of memory. However, in many instances, it is not memory loss, but loss of some recall capacity. For example, a person will be talking and will suddenly not be able to recall a familiar name. If the attention is turned elsewhere for a few seconds or minutes, the sought-after name will flash into the mind. When this happens, it indicates that the memory is still there, but the available recall circuits are temporarily busy.

Our memory resources are very adaptable to changing needs. For instance, there are enormous amounts of information which the mind judges to be inconsequential data. These are filed away at both the conscious and unconscious levels. Soon, if the information does not need to be recalled, it becomes irretrievable by the conscious mind.

Adroit students carrying heavy university course loads usually learn to organize the mind's memory-forgetting processes. Detail material, which is considered important to remember only until the next major exam, will be filed in the memory with that instruction. Other data which is thought to be necessary for the pursuit of one's career for many years ahead, will be reviewed several times and either hooked into the memory for long-term recall, or clearly identified as to the reference book where it may be reread.

Unless one has a photographic memory, or intends to win TV quiz shows, one does not clutter the brain with endless trivia.

The Brain Damage of Complacency

Like your body's voluntary muscles, your brain cells are meant to be used. When they are used intelligently, when they are exercised and cared for, the brain cells tend to maintain their capacity and their power to be of service. Some people dread the possibility of getting old and losing their mental alertness, almost as though those two events were inevitably linked together. No one is going to halt the eventual consequences of aging. However, if we take the trouble to be observant, we see that a large percent of the population begins to limit itself artificially and unnecessarily early in adulthood *by simply ceasing to exercise their brains.*

The time to begin doing something about that problem is *now.*

It is hard to exaggerate the risk of mind impairment which may be caused by mental laziness, stereotyped thinking, and lack of mental exercise. Over a period of years these habits can produce damage comparable to the effects of some brain diseases or accidents. Few disabilities are more tragic to observe than the self-induced mental rigidities and atrophied mental equipment of persons who are faced with a need to change their life patterns and have lost the brain's capacity to make the necessary adjustment. Whenever this happens to any of us, our relatives and close associates often undergo acute and sudden frustration. They do not know what to say or do to help us.

A professional associate developed this kind of problem. It was a pitiful thing to observe a brilliant, inquisitive mind closing its windows rapidly. And yet, in his case there was no brain disease nor physically caused brain damage.

He had enjoyed stimulating mental activity during youth and early adult years. At a major university his broader interests in art, literature and culture were developed. Early on, he discovered and cultivated a talent for innovative sales work. In middle years, circumstances moved him into a situation of great family stress. At first, he took steps to extricate himself. But later, some inner motive led him into similar relationships of overstress. Soon he began to reduce his broader interests. He settled into a narrowing response of standardized cliches, centered around the least inventive of his lucrative, sales techniques.

Apparently, he lost all capacity to respond in a fresh, creative way to new ideas. The remainder of his life was spent within the self-created cocoon, where there was decreasing mental resources for emergence.

Maintenance of stimulating mental activity can reduce the risk of such impairment. Regular, enjoyable physical exercise is now recognized to be a basic need if one is to maintain good health. *Regular, enjoyable mental exercise is a part of brain care and maintenance.*

Exercise the Curiosity

Little children tend to possess the quality of curiosity. The most alert adults retain a large capacity for curiosity throughout their lives, since they *never stop practicing* its use. However, most of us tend to be inquisitive only about certain things. We tend to stop inquiring about events or objects outside our daily range. One reason, no doubt, is that we get so very busy doing whatever is needed. Another reason we sometimes give is, "I am not interested; that subject is of no use to me." In other instances, we may have had our curiosity turned off by adults who were impatient with us in our early school years.

Whatever the causes, most people along the way lose some of what my parents called, "our children's curiosity bumps." (They were referring to a common notion of the time that certain irregularities on the skull indicated one's mental potentials.)

Curiosity, in its purest form, is the desire to know for the sake of knowing, not for advantage, not for any immediate gain, but simply to be familiar with the territory of one's universe. Asking, "Why?" not in desperation, but in wonder and with the capacity to be surprised is an essential function of the mind's potential for fantasy, imagination and youthful growth.

A Suggested Exercise

At occasions in my own life, when there has come a mental hint of staleness, one exercise has never failed to provide a remedy. I would set aside a few hours or a half day when a trip could be made to a public library. Starting with some subject of interest, preferably one which had not been explored for a time, I would go to the nonfiction sections and browse through the shelves. Soon a book would arouse further curiosity. I might spend the rest of the time reading in it. Or, I might be stimulated to browse further through the shelves. Possibly, I would go to the card files to look for a specific subject and then go back to the bookcases.

Usually, a new vista would open to my imagination. The ideas and experiences of an author new to me would be shared. Often, I might check out two or three volumes to take home for more reading at my leisure.

Another Exercise

Some people find it easier to begin the restimulation of curiosity through conversation, rather than reading. A close friend is like that. For him, reading about a subject is usually his final step in exploring it. He talks to a few people. He asks questions about individuals who may be knowledgeable about a topic of interest to him. Then, he contacts a wider circle of these and asks more questions. The process by which he retains a curious mind through conversation is as continuous in all his social contacts as is the process I customarily tend to use with books.

The particular method one uses for remaining mentally alert is apparently not as important as establishing a habit of doing something innovative. One simply has to get into the habit of using techniques, such as those suggested above, to refuel and restimulate the brain periodically. When it comes to exercise, nothing happens usually by accident. We have to do something for ourselves, or inertia does us in.

Also, we can usually expand and make better use of the resources of the unconscious mind. The advantages of the intuitive, unconscious brain powers are

1. the ability to draw upon memory resources which are astronomically larger than those of the conscious mind, and
2. the great speed of the intuitive brain in analyzing this body of complex data.

Working alone, the conscious mind cannot usually solve extremely complex, original problems, except through use of library research, mathematical formulas, and laborious effort. In everyday life many individuals have found that cultivation of both logical and intuitive types of thought contributes to personal enjoyment. If the mind is kept in balance through the methods we have suggested throughout this volume, the accuracy of insights from the intuitive, unconscious levels can be given a high degree of trust.

You can exercise the mind by using the conscious mind to check the practicality and persistence of the hunches coming from your unconscious levels. As you become more experienced in sorting genuine hunches out from the more transient wishes or fears, you will gain skill in knowing when to base decisions upon a combination of both levels feeding you data in harmony. When you learn to recognize a genuine hunch, trust it. As the Quakers and practical mystics have taught us, when we learn to follow our Leadings, we are given more Leadings.

Any unconscious impulse which would alienate one from ethical responsibilities or block one's capacity to give and receive love should not be followed. In the jargon of some recovery groups, when a person fills the unconscious with anger, resentment, fear, false guilt, or egocentricity, one is not "keeping one's head screwed on properly." With the unconscious mind filled and colored with such negative, self-centered feelings, its motivations and assessments are destructive and distorted.

Maintenance and care of the brain must include the regular therapeutic disciplines of putting those feelings into the mind which are the true expression of what it means to be a *whole person.* It is not enough to make a new beginning of understanding the self, and committing the life to a Power greater than oneself. These orientations must be *continued* and provided with opportunities for *growth.*

There is another feature of our brains, which provides a safeguard against burning out the finely-tuned organ. Individuals who work with other people in enjoyable, stimulating positions will find themselves experiencing a unique type of fatigue.

My first personal encounter with this problem occurred while working as director of a department for a national health agency based in New York City. There was a high degree of daily stimulation in our work. We never knew what kind of exciting, interesting problem might be presented on the telephone or by someone coming to the office by appointment. Those of us on the staff teams enjoyed our assignments, but found that periodic mental fatigue of overstimulation would occur.

Whenever a new staff person was employed, part of the orientation was preparation for this special kind of exhaustion and how to cope with it. The new person would be told something as follows:

After you have been with us two or three months, some Friday afternoon you will go home feeling unusually tired. Saturday morning you will still feel tired. You may wonder why you are not rested after a good night's sleep.

So, you will lie around and do rather routine, easy things on Saturday. You will probably feel like getting to bed fairly early that evening. But Sunday morning you will awaken still feeling uninterested in everything and vaguely tired.

You may begin to wonder whether you are coming down with the flu, but your only symptoms seem to be a lack of your usual pep and enthusiasm. After another good night's sleep, you will probably awaken with your customary energy and mental interest on Monday morning.

We found that several weeks after employment, the new staff person would report one Monday morning that the kind of experience described above had occurred over the past weekend. With a sheepish grin, the individual would also admit that until then there had been some disbelief about the earlier orientation.

As a follow-up, the person would be told to expect such periods of disinterest and fatigue quite often. Also, he or she would be advised that the best remedy, if an episode should occur in the middle of the workweek, was to reschedule a couple of days which could be spent in routine desk work. Insofar as possible, people contacts should be delegated to other staff members.

This type of fatigue is sometimes mistaken for "burn out." It is actually merely the brain's response to sustained overstimulation and overenjoyment of one's work. The brain shuts down part of its circuitry until a period of respite from the overstimulation can take place. Subsequently, the "circuit breaker" cuts back in and the person is again ready to resume the enjoyable functions.

We possess an intricate and beautiful instrument of thought, which includes conscious and unconscious levels, huge memory resources, and built-in protectors against overloading its circuits.

With appreciation for these resources, limitations, and processes we are in a better position to maintain and care for the brain.

CHAPTER 10
RETIREMENT: RETREATING, RESHUFFLING, OR ELECTIVE YEARS

The crisis of retirement is different from most others which may present the need to begin anew. This event is usually not unexpected.

There are some exceptions, of course. A total disability retirement often comes with a sudden injury or illness. Early retirement pay is sometimes offered to eligible employees when jobs are terminated or economic conditions cause permanent layoffs within a company. But the usual retirement is one type of major life change which gives us time for advance planning.

Retirement can be one of the more exciting, satisfying periods of one's life. But, the occasion may become one long, oblong blur of disasters. Whether a person lands at one extreme or the other — or somewhere in the middle — largely depends upon how well the advance plans are made.

As I review the experiences of my peers, there are three problem areas we all face. The first two are stereotypes and assumptions we carry around in our heads. The third problem is something in which the cultural notions (mystique) of society wrap us.

These are

1. stereotypes about retirement as a time of retreating and resting, of continuous vacation, or a time for hobby and volunteer activities,

2. assumptions that our health/energy level is going to remain at about the present level for a considerable time, and

3. society's subtle inducements to put retirees "on the shelf," to exaggerate the value of youth, and to play the games of aging-denial.

Once we have looked at the substance of these ideas and folklore, we can more easily lay their ghosts to rest. Alternative approaches to the retirement period will then open before us in exciting ways. We shall find our way more directly through the tangle of confusing advice about

- what should one do with the retirement years?
- where should one live?
- how about financing?

Stereotypes About Retirement

The most frequent comment heard by busy, creative retirees is, "But you're not *really* retired." The remark is meant as a compliment. However, it reveals how prevalent is the stereotype in society of retirement as a period in one's older years which should be devoted to retreating and resting. The word, itself, contributes to the continuation of the stereotype. When one "retires" it is *from* something.

The common notion is that when you reach retirement you can *get away* from your line of work, your occupation, or your employer. You will then receive a pension to supplement your savings and provide the financial support to permit you to be free of work. You will be able to sit back in a rocking chair to enjoy a well-earned rest from the long years of productivity.

Another meaning of retiring is to go to bed in preparation for sleep at night.

These stereotypes are distortions of what should properly happen when people qualify for their pensions. For most individuals, there are few conditions less healthful and more boring than an endless period of resting without having any useful function to perform.

The stereotypes kill a lot of people earlier than they should die!

In partial recognition that years of extended idleness and rest are not truly good for us, many individuals take what they feel to be a more positive viewpoint. They think of retirement as a time of endless, but very active, vacation.

The so-called retirement village advertising caters to this notion. They promote the virtues of their project as a recreational dream location. There will be pictures of active, energetic people over age 55 enjoying the golf courses, tennis courts, swimming pools, bicycle trails, or what have you.

Another picture which comes to mind is of the vast travel facilities and resources that have been developed for retirees in recent years. Couples who have not had sufficient time or opportunity during the steadily employed years for travel will often welcome the new opportunity to see their own continent's beauties.

Some people will purchase a trailer or motor home and spend an extended period in seminomadic exploration of scenic areas they have never thoroughly enjoyed. Others become avid world travelers. Still others become involved in a combination of travel and education through programs such as Elderhostel. There is an almost endless choice of options, scaled to fit a wide variety of budgets. Such activities can be very satisfying, especially if the way of life does not become so exclusively occupying that individuals fail to develop alternative activities through which they perform services useful to others.

A further broadening of the activity theme occurs with people who view retirement as a time to pursue hobby interests, to develop new ones, or to engage in voluntary work suitable to their tastes. With imagination, a collection of such activities can comprise a useful and satisfying lifestyle.

Whether the retirement years are a time of real fulfillment or whether they slide into a long decline of boredom and frustration will depend, largely, upon the mental attitude with which one approaches this period of life. There are legitimate needs for more resting during the older years, as well as a more flexible time schedule for hobby and recreational activities. The important distinction between taking the route of boredom or the path of fulfillment perhaps lies in whether one views retirement years as

1. an empty space to be filled somehow, or
2. as a unique opportunity to do useful things one would deeply enjoy doing.

As an alternative to the retreating or reshuffling approaches, I suggest looking upon this *beginning* as a time of choices.

The Elective Years

In a pamphlet about aging there was a quotation some years ago from a person named Joe Hudson, who lived in Gibson City, Illinois. I liked his statement so much that I copied it into one of my notebooks. Mr. Hudson was reported to have said, "I'm not a senior citizen — I'm a *seasoned* citizen, I'm not in my retirement years — I'm in my *elective* years."[1]

Don't you like that thought? A "seasoned citizen" in his "elective years." A person whom the prior years and experiences have seasoned, toughened, and made resilient. A person who has reached that point in life where he or she can not only choose areas of service and activity involvement, but has also become mature enough to make those decisions wisely.

One is reminded of a statement from one of the ancient Apocryphal books, *The Wisdom of Sirach*:[2]

A well-taught man knows a great deal,
A man of experience will discourse with understanding.
The man who has not been tested, knows little,
But the man who has wandered far gains great ingenuity.

When our granddaughter reached the age of eight, she had learned the multiplication tables. Proudly, she was giving us the answers to questions of what is six times seven, four times eight, and so on. Her newly acquired skill was the beginning of a knowledge. However, she would spend many more years learning how to apply that skill. Only as her knowledge became seasoned and used would she achieve understanding of the scope and limitations of the multiplication tables.

So it is with every area of information. We do not truly know anything until we have used it for survival, for enjoyment, for service, for growth. Information skills only become knowledge and wisdom when they have been seasoned with experience, with value judgments, and through years of personal testing.

All of us who have reached the elective years have come to them through the years of seasoning. So what? There is little satisfaction in that, unless we find ways now to function fruitfully. The focus of our choices, at any age, about vocations and avocations should always be upon the questions, "What are my priorities? How do I choose the highest quality among the multiplicity of possible activities?"

The trouble is that during our middle years we often feel forced by accident or economic necessity to choose those activities that paid for the house or put food on the table.

Now, we do not need any longer to limit our activities to those which pay well, or which provide security, or those that afford us status. We can do volunteer work in a print shop because it may be fun; we can take lessons on the cello without being concerned whether we ever make the concert stage. We can knit or sew or study Spanish without giving a second thought to whether others think we are using our time wisely. We can tutor a child who is slow in a school project or show a grandson how to build a kite. We can operate a part-time bookkeeping business, or repair the church's mimeograph machine, or keep diaries, or make crossword puzzles for sale to magazines. We can collect historical information and write books or articles about it. The variety of things we *can* do is as broad as our skills, and the *new skills* we can *acquire*.

The necessities of the middle years also require us to put much emphasis upon the quantity we produce. In those years, we may not be doing exactly what we most enjoy doing, but we get the economic message that we had better do a lot of it! The problems occur for us at the point where we imagine our worth is linked to our capacity to produce a large volume of something or to engage in many activities, regardless of other considerations.

The focus of the elective years can be upon the *quality* of one's activity; enjoyment of one's functions and new learning experiences; the opportunity to taste, to savor, to appreciate the elements of life; and the freedom to serve with love.

But also, the focus needs to be upon the opportunities for *new choices*. The elective years! What an exciting time of life it can be. A time when one can bring all the years' experience and seasoning to bear upon today's activities, today's joys, today's quality.

Yet, in these years we may be tripped up by a false assumption. We must not assume that we can depend in years ahead upon REMAINING AS HEALTHY AS TO-DAY.

Realistic Health Expectations

This is not a realistic assumption after we reach the sixties, even for those who feel extraordinarily vigorous. It is an okay assumption for a nineteen-year-old person deciding upon a career choice or a selection of a higher educational goal. But to begin one's planning for the older years with the idea that physical potential and mobility will remain about on a plateau can be costly and often danger-ous. Yet, when considering activity options and residential locations, it is often tragic to observe how many retirees make inappropriate choices. They often seem to feel it is a sign of being in charge to avoid looking at realities of the aging process.

In my opinion, the reason so many people fail to question the basic assumption of their continued health level is simply because of habit. They have been accustomed for many years to a gradual decline of physical powers. They have learned to adjust to that. But it simply does not occur to them that now the time of life has been reached when the risks of rather sharp declines are much greater.

For example, in choosing residences, one observes pensioners investing in residences large enough to entertain the occasional visits of the entire collection of offspring and grandchildren. They will lock themselves into such real estate investments at a time when more flexible housing would be desirable. Leasing a smaller place and putting their capital funds into solid income securities might give them a better option, if serious illness or accident made care of a large house a burden.

Choices of activities, as well as residence, can also go awry. A married couple took their Social Security pensions at age 65 and moved from the Midwest to a milder, sun-belt climate. He had worked as a skilled auto body shop man. She had much office experience in both general filing and typing, as well as manager in small establishments. He assumed he could continue to do body and painting work independently on a reduced scale. If necessary, she planned to secure part-time office work. However, he had never developed any avocations or more sedentary types of interests. He never saw any need for such broadening of activity.

They got along well for three or four years. Then, he began to develop severe arthritic symptoms that made it impossible to use the tools of his trade. As his health deteriorated further, she found that leaving home for regular part-time office work was becoming increasingly difficult.

The couple did have enough pension and income from savings to cover basic expenses, but a very unsatisfactory marital existence developed. Problems which had long lurked close to the surface, now became aggravated with both of them together continuously in a small house.

Yet, they were bound to one another by economic necessity. Neither of them had formed regular habits of outside activity in behalf of others, nor any options for income supplement that might have provided more flexibility.

These two people both had some very pleasant, agreeable qualities, but they were locked into a pattern of increasing frustration. Their situation was typical of so many other couples, since their options had been closed by lifelong habits. They had drifted along on the assumption that the energy reserves to make major changes would always be there, if needed.

The elective years provide opportunities for exciting new choices. They also carry the implicit need to plan and choose wisely for the certainty that the future will bring, at some points, reduced physical energy. There is a frequent and pathetic phrase often repeated when older people consider an opportunity to sell the large house they occupy and move to a smaller, more adaptable retirement accommodation. The cliche one hears so frequently is, "We are not ready." By this is really meant, "We still have our mobility. If we make such a move now, people may think we are *really* old."

Let's try to take an honest look at that. What about this youth mystique? Why are we so entranced by the notion that youth is our ideal? Why do we permit the mystique and its subtle notions to complicate and often endanger our fullest enjoyment of the later years? According to statistical averages, we have about seventeen years after we reach age sixty-five. That is a sizable chunk of time — worth the effort to plan well toward making the period a satisfying one.

Aging-Denial Games

The clues to existence of any social mystique are perhaps best seen in the alibi-denial games we play to avoid reality. So, look at the age sixty-five and above group. One might think such individuals had come to terms with themselves as people. Yet, we observe many of them still playing a familiar game associated with birthdays. It is revealed by a set of common cliches, such as

"I'm age thirty-nine."

"Forty-nine and holding."

"Sixty-two, and no more birthdays."

Just what is supposedly so great about age 62, or 49, or 39?

Another game involves a greeting between two older persons. It takes a variety of individual forms, but the following is an example:

"I haven't seen you for some while. My, you look great!"

"Well, you do too," comes the response. "You're only as old as you feel, I always say."

Notice how the subject of youth and age sneaked into this conversational exchange. To see the absurdity, shift the scene to an imagined meeting of two persons in their early twenties:

"Hi, I haven't seen you since high school. You look good."

"Well, like they say, 'If you think sixteen, you'll look sixteen.' "

Another game, with a more desperate tone, occurs when individuals talk about how long they might enjoy living. Someone invariably visualizes the most depressing scenario of a person who has gone into a state of advanced senility, or a helpless bedfast condition after a severe stroke.

Then, the line goes something as follows:

"I don't want to live that long."

Of course not. No one would wish that, under those circumstances. But notice how the lines are always played from the mystique theme. One never hears it said, "I would hope I never become ill in that way before I die." Instead, the expression is usually attached to the *aging level.*

It is in the manner we express ourselves that we betray our emotional hang-ups and our social mystique assumptions.

The implication is that there is something inherently disagreeable and undesirable about getting older, more so, that is, than about the problems of any other age period.

Nonsense.

It is possible to be trapped in situations of copelessness within any age level.

It is true that there are some problems of the older years which require degrees of toughness and tempering sometimes beyond the comprehension of the young or the middle-aged. However, in the balance of things, older folks also have the potential advantage of richer experience/understanding with which to cope. In the older years one does not *have to remain* prone to all the mistakes and pitfalls of the younger years!

In looking at the reality of the older years, it is good practical sense to plan for the certainty of aging.

Declining Energy Level

Anytime, of course, during the years after 60 there may be considerable periods when health and energy remain level, or even show improvement. But plan flexibly so that your options will be available if and when health declines unexpectedly.

A friend, who was a skilled pattern maker in the machine tool business, knew that the time of pensions and retirement would one day take him from work he loved and did so well.

He planned for that time and for the fact that declining physical endurance would probably make it desirable to keep more of his activity at home. Several years before his retirement date, he began to augment his basement shop with various tools which would permit him to do more small work with woods, metals, and plastics. While still employed steadily, and able to invest in future equipment, he built a dune buggy, including an all-weather plastic body. Since he had never undertaken this kind of project before, it was an excellent investment in explorng his own interests and in testing what basement shop equipment would be most useful to him after retirement.

Out of these activities and explorations, including extensive reading of mechanical-crafts journals, he developed several new interests. So, when pension collection time arrived, he was ready for it with a flexible set of useful and fun things. With the exception of total disabihty, he had his plans designed to fit any energy level. They will probably give him fulfillment for the remainder of his life.

Some time before age 65, a Department of Interior employee bought a cottage for weekend and summer use in a historic area of Virginia. He became interested in the local history and began to collect notes about the origin of place-names — towns, crossroads, streams.

The hobby began to blossom into a major activity for the retirement years. He began to be systematic in seeking information about the background of these place-names, tracing their origin through old town and church records, library archives, and family records of the area.

After beginning to receive pensions, the searches and notetaking became the kind of thing which he perceived as a flexible and continuing pursuit for which there was a demand in various new publications.

In the early years of retirement, he had a variety of community activities. As physical vigor slowly declined, he focused more upon the more sedentary place-names research. On days when he felt vigorous and the weather was good, he could go on field trips for information. On other occasions, he could digest and organize the materials at home. The mix of various activities provided him with satisfying outlets, which continued for the remainder of his life.

The Second Big Decision

After a married couple or a single person has decided what kind of activities should fill the elective years, there is a second big decision.

Then, they need to determine the best location to live for these years and these activities. Many individuals make the choice of a place to retire their *first* priority. They pick a place for its climate or its scenery or because their grown children live nearby. After that choice, they often discover that the climate or scenery area does not happen to posses opportunities to do things they truly like. Or, there are poor medical and transportation facilities where the beautiful scenery is located. Or, when they get settled, the young folk get job offers so attractive that they regretfully move halfway across the continent.

In our first illustration of the former pattern maker, the couple found that their best location was the familiar, manageable residence where they had lived for over thirty years.

The former government employee found that the weekend cottage area provided the best activity center. And his wife had developed two major interests which could also be best followed in that setting, rather than the city. Her interests, likewise, were such that they could be reduced with time to fit her energy.

A Tip for Financial Planning

Many individuals have their financial planning and reserves for the contingencies of inflation well in hand by the time of retirement. But for others, it is necessary to give considerable attention to income and budget.

Plans for supplementing income can be one resource. Another is the use of lifelong skills in keeping expenses at a minimum. A third resource is inherent in the fact that, as needed, retirees can arrange things so that living costs are considerably lower than they were during the steady working years.

However, many people find that using the elective years concept in planning is financially advantageous. The person has chosen to be occupied creatively with enjoyable things. If supplemental income is needed later on, it is more apt to be found by the individual who is involved happily, than by those who simply drift into a part-time job.

Second, the contacts with a community of involved persons is usually greater for those who get active in creative things. Then, if one needs contacts and friends, they are already present.

Someone has facetiously said, "Retirement is that time of life when you know all the answers, but nobody asks you." However, those of us who are busily involved in doing happy, needed things discover we are not easily forgotten. So, the retirement planning experts agree that one should first decide

1. what to do with your time,
2. where to reside that will be most suitable, and only then
3. focus major attention upon how to arrange for it financially.

In the retirement-planning literature, which is increasing rapidly, stories abound of people who were surprised at how well they got along financially when they followed that sequence and began their planning several years in advance of retirement date.

What About Resource Materials?

The amount of information available is truly amazing, at least to those few of us who have been interested in the subject since the middle of this century. Publication of good material began to increase rapidly during the 1970s. By 1980 any large public library contained shelves of books on aging and retirement. Many more people are now giving attention to planning. But the bad news is that too many individuals are still not facing the issue soon enough.

The *good news* is that in increasing numbers more people are experiencing the fun of using their acquired skills and ingenuity to develop ways of remaining useful within today's society.

CHAPTER 11
WHAT ZESTFUL OLDSTERS
CAN TEACH US

Why should we have an interest in learning anything from old people?

People of all ages should listen closely to a certain segment of the older group — the *zestful* survivors in that population. They are a rich source of wisdom, since they possess a vast store of experience in coping with every conceivable life problem and crisis.

Some concerned people have been saying that older citizens represent an increasing percentage of the population, so everyone should listen more carefully to the oldsters. Also, among the politicians and lobbyists there are voices which call for giving pensioners a larger share of the government benefits. Some older citizens are encountering serious problems that need public attention. To be sure, older people have often been nudged out of the mainstream. But merely emphasizing the so-called rights of older people leaves some of us with a feeling of imbalance.

On the other side of the scales is the obligation, and the privilege, of oldsters to resume their proper role of making vital contributions to the larger community. As more and more of them are doing that, some of the younger and middle-aged people are listening attentively.

Even today we are just beginning to appreciate how much we can learn about survival and significance from some of these older citizens.

Among those who survive with spunkiness well into their seventies and beyond, one can observe five common characteristics:

1. They try to enjoy everything with humor, including their own foibles and follies.
2. They fight for every ounce of life, but do not flinch from the approach of death. They are not docile.
3. They do everything today that one can do, but they go with life's flow. They live with comfortable self-discipline and moderation.
4. Their zest is a personal affirmation that old age is as much an alive time as childhood, youth, or the middle years.
5. Their good emotional patterns of younger years have set up mental programs for the years of less energy and narrowing options.

Zest is a common characteristic of these folk. There is a certain kind of twinkle that one frequently sees in their eyes.

Another evidence of their attitudes is seen in a lifestyle questionnaire that has been widely used in recent years by researchers at university centers for the study of gerontology.

In administering the questionnaire the procedure is to give it to a representative sample of older citizens and to follow up with the same group a few years later after the onset of greater physical activity reduction. An example of such a reduction would be the need to give up driving one's own car.[1]

Each time the survey has been conducted it has clearly shown that individuals who cope well and are happy with their life situations tend to remain content with their lives in the declining years.

Without attempting to evaluate deeply the causes of this observed experience, it is apparent from the interviews that people who remain content are those who, in their younger years, acquired lifestyles of growth, spunk, and serenity regarding themselves and their universe. These patterns had not only become habitual, but could apparently withstand the test of adversity.

The health problems and mobility limitations among some of these individuals in the surveys became so great that it would not be remarkable if the experiences had soured their dispositions. But, almost without exception, those who had confronted life with a high degree of enjoyment in more comfortable years were the ones who were capable of sustaining that personality tone in time of greater adversity.

A Sense of Humor and the Will to Live

The will to live and a keen sense of humor seem to be closely linked in all zestful older persons. When they encounter serious life-threatening illnesses or injuries, this blending of humor and stubborn fight for life is especially noticeable.

By sense of humor we mean here the capacity to laugh at oneself. We sometimes think that readiness to grasp the point of a joke indicates that a person has a sense of humor. Not necessarily.

For instance, my own mother never cared much for jokes, puns, or quips. It wasn't because she missed their point. Instead, she appeared to be somewhat bored with such humor. Her underlying, truly hilarious reactions to life events were most obvious in the later years past age ninety when her current memory span had shrunk to about three or four minutes. At that stage she had difficulty coping with more than the most elementary of crossword puzzles. To remember a long horizontal word in a puzzle, while searching for a matching one on the vertical file was impossible.

When we visited at the care center, where she and Papa were then residing, Mama's greeting was, "Am I supposed to know you?"

This was always said with twinkling eyes and a broad smile. Later, whenever I left on some errand and returned to them in a few minutes, Mama would ask, again with a twinkle. "Were you here before?"

Thus, she got her bearings on whom and when, but did it in a way that also said, in effect, "This memory loss is a terrible thing, but I want you to share in my joke about it."

An important element in humor is its capacity to see the funny, ridiculous side of the most serious situations. In recent years we seem to have been developing a pathetic trend in this country. We often hear it said that such-and-such a topic is too serious to joke about. Have such critics failed to note that the funniest jokes involve the most serious topics — death, marital crises, disasters? Without our capacity to laugh at ourselves we could only be people deficient in objectivity and in the will to survive.

The zestful oldsters have cultivated this art. It is an important part of their survival resources. Two of our older friends and neighbors are Edward and Ruth Demson. We have known them well for about a decade. At present writing, he is past age 90.

"Jed," as he likes to be called by his friends, since those are the initials of his names, passed his bar examinations and practiced law for a time in Cleveland, Ohio. Then, he and Ruth moved to California where Dr. Demson became a member of the faculty of Stanford University Law School until he reached normal retirement age.

Moving then to Phoenix, Arizona, he taught for several more years on the law faculty at Arizona State University in Tempe. After another retirement from that assignment, he began to write a regular newspaper column in which he answered legal inquiries of readers by researching what the law said in their localities. He had continued that activity at home until quite recently, when physical energy finally declined below the level to sustain the newspaper work.

When about age 85, he told me of devices he used to cope with declining memory span. For example, when he

went to the law library in later years to research certain
questions from readers, he could no longer depend upon
memory to last from the study table until he walked to the
book stacks a short distance away. He would write a note
to himself, which he carried to the bookshelves. Then, he
would write the answer on the paper and carry it back to
the study table. This was told with a twinkle in his eye. It
was amusing to him, and he felt we should share in the
irony of it.

Another story he told with great relish a few years ago
concerns a morning when he met their paper boy making
the regular delivery. Jed stepped outside just as the young
fellow dropped the paper on the porch. He said to the boy,
"Please put the paper on this porch chair. I'm getting too
old to stoop down for it on the floor." (Actually, he was
then still able to stoop and do considerable gardening work
among his flower beds.)

"How old are you, mister?" asked the lad.

"I'm 84," replied Dr. Demson, standing erectly and
sturdily by his front door.

The boy's eyes widened in surprise. "My gawd!" he
exclaimed.[2]

Another friend and neighbor is Robert J. Hannelly. He is
a mathematician by training and was President of Phoenix
College and President of the Maricopa County Community
College District prior to his retirement. An outstanding
community leader, yet perhaps in the quality of life his
equal contribution has been the demonstration of resilience
and humor during the crises of personal illness and accident in later years.

For a class in creative writing, Bob recently wrote a short
piece called "The View From Eighty-Two." With his permission two quotations from that are appropriate here:

It makes a difference whether one is in the active
seventies, the tired eighties, or the near-heaven nine-
ties. There are many removable parts such as teeth,

spectacles, and hearing aids. One friend said he had more spare parts than Phoenix's largest auto dealer. . . . Walking is a chore, but it must be done. If one can think and move, he has it made.

Family affairs are of very great importance to old people. One loves his children dearly, but should never make the mistake to live with one of them. Grandchildren are no longer cute and cuddly. They may have whiskers or be married. Adult sons and daughters are busy and shouldn't be bothered by oldsters. However from time to time they feel constrained to get the old parents "organized." After they are through with this job and have gone, it's no great problem to arrange the household as it was before. However, it is impossible to recover clothes they gave to Goodwill Industries.[3]

Dr. Hannelly's comments are typical of the thread of sly humor one hears throughout the daily conversations of older people who live with zest.

The Meek, Not the Docile, Shall Inherit the Earth

We have gotten somewhat confused in our culture about the distinctions between the meaning of being docile, meek, and humble.

Zestful older people continuously demonstrate that people who are docile and submissive are not the best survivors. Furthermore, docile individuals are apt to have tremendous repressed resentments within them. One might even go a step further to conclude it is wise to beware of the overly nice person.

The word "meek," as it is used in older English translations of the New Testament, conveys something a little different from the original Greek. The New English Bible translates it "of gentle spirit." However, my personal preference has long been for a French translation which uses the word "debonair."

158

To be debonair means to be a gentleman or gentlewoman — a person with consideration for others and a sense of identity of oneself. It implies a sense of humor, a style of living with both objectivity and involvement. It suggests an individual who is at home with self and who has a sense of membership in the human family.

Such a person is not docile; neither is there a need to be overly self-assertive. One is in balance.

With that understanding, we can see how such persons are inheritors of the earth. The qualities we have been describing enable persons at any age level to acquire excellent tools in making a good fight for every ounce of life. Without flinching, these individuals can contemplate the death which awaits us all.

Becoming an *inheritor* of the creativeness we experience on earth is a quality of the spirit. Quite a different thing it is from striving to be a *possessor* of the earth and its goods. The distinction is between becoming a part of life and trying to own pieces of life's turf.

Comfortable Self-Discipline

A unique distinction among zestful oldsters is their comfortable style of self-discipline.

Since these older folks are in touch with themselves, they tend to be adept at staying within the boundaries of their individual limits. Moderation in activity, food, drink, exercise and emotional tone is the rule among them, rather than the exception.

The one area over which everyone has the greatest potential control is himself. The old ones change what they can, themselves.

Being zestful and self-disciplined will not guarantee longevity. However, if one persists in living *without* humor, enjoyment, and discipline, one's life span will likely be shortened and certainly be a bore. By the time a person has gotten into the eighties, the peer group is almost entirely composed of zestful, self-disciplined people. Most of the others are dead already! The only exceptions are a small percentage who chose their grandparents exceedingly well or who are surviving with expensive life support systems of one kind or another.

Obviously, the self-discipline of the oldster is not like that of the religious ascetic. There is no flagellation, either with whips or mental self-blame, and little deprivation. Rather, it is a way of life focused upon creating a mode of true comfort. The objective is a lifestyle that is an easy fit with oneself.

Built around moderation, the oldster attempts to augment the ability to function well for today and also for the longer haul. One tries to arrange eating habits so that there is balanced nutrition in menus which agree with the individual digestive processes. Physical exercise is regular and is apt to involve the activities of walking or swimming. Rest periods are also regular and ample for the person's needs. If an afternoon or morning nap is helpful in remaining functional, the person will probably try to include these rests in the daily pattern.

There is no standard formula. Usually each individual has worked out a personal style and established the discipline to maintain that routine. However, once a workable style has been tested and adopted, the person will usually be very independent and tenacious in following it under almost any circumstances, whether at home or on a visit out of town.

In general, this approach is also useful to anyone, at any age, who is rebuilding after a serious life crisis.

As we have seen earlier, it is necessary in making a new beginning

1. to have a center of inner quiet,
2. to be in charge of one's life, and
3. to change the changeable.

In all three of these areas, the oldsters' techniques of comfortable self-discipline are instructive.

First, the older person takes care to preserve an inner center of quiet, wherein decisions essential to the self are made, executed, and evaluated.

Second, the seasoned citizen takes care to be independently in charge of his or her private decisions. There is certainly gentleness and tolerance with associates, but the seasoned persons do not surrender control, simply to be agreeable. Long since, they learned to say, "No." And they can say it very sweetly, but firmly. Long ago, they learned that when they eat something, it is their systems which must digest it, not someone else's intestinal tract! So, they usually eat what agrees with them, not something which another person urges upon them.

They put out the energy which is proper for them to expend in a given time and do not permit themselves to become overfatigued because of overcommitment.

Third, they will focus strictly upon those things which can and should be changed. They have learned that there are some problems for which there are no feasible solutions and many more for which they no longer have sufficient time, even if they know the solutions. To a degree beyond the practice of many younger people, they are strict with themselves about the day-to-day implementation of those criteria.

However, if you are a younger person making a new beginning after a life crisis, may I make a suggestion. Locate a bright-eyed, zestful oldster who seems unapproachable in your community. Invite that person's comments upon the issues, priorities, and decisions you are making. If you find someone like that with whom you have rapport, you will acquire a mentor — a person who will listen and give you support.

We should not make the mistake of thinking that these folks are rigid and inflexible. If there is truly a need for a major change, and it is within their power to make that alteration, they can often be observed to move with amazing speed. The reason for such great adaptability in older years is that long ago they learned to be adept at accepting the circumstances which they could *not* change. They are realists of the first order!

In contrast to the picture of comfortable self-discipline we have been describing is the general society in which we live. It is a society full of distraught and annoying noises.

The Frantic Lifestyle

As an illustration, recently I thought it would be interesting to listen for the noises, rather than the messages, of a half-hour news section being broadcast on a national network station. It was a revealing experience: the so-called background music of the news and the commercials, various rapid sound effects, the injection of insistent voices, the changes in pitch, the striking contrasts designed to get attention.

One grows accustomed to this cascade of sound and gradually becomes somewhat oblivious to most of the vibrations assaulting the eardrums. There is a mish-mash of tones, voices in local dialects, doggerel verse, ungrammatical half-sentences, all of it delivered with a rapid-fire, kaleidoscopic, quick-flash impact. Then, of course, there is the usual young weather reporter, who delivers his lines in fast-speak. (One wonders what percentage increase of high blood pressure will be reported among these rapid talkers by the time they reach 1995.)

I switched off the rest of program to finish lunch in quiet, and another illustration came to mind.

A little earlier in the day, we were driving across town on an avenue running near our residence. There are streetlights spaced about every half-mile along this avenue. They are synchronized for a steady speed between 35 and 40 miles per hour. It is a busy route, but since there are three lanes each way, the traffic is not excessively heavy by urban standards.

Yet, about half of the drivers were engaged in their usual thoughtless practice of getting away from a stop with speed and braking hard when they arrived at the next streetlight too soon. It is not an easy, comfortable kind of driving.

I recall experiences while living in Manhattan of riding with some of the better taxi and limousine drivers in the New York City area, admiring the disciplined skill with which they observed traffic and lights far ahead. In contrast to less competent drivers, they had great ability to maintain a steady pace, which ate up miles rapidly in all except the most heavily congested traffic.

It is encouraging to note that there are thoughtful, seasoned individuals among us, not all of them older people, who have learned to live with calmness, even in the midst of near-chaos. The purpose of self-discipline is to keep inner-directed, rather than permit all the external, frantic voices to push us away from the paths of our intentions.

Why are some of these oldsters so zestful?

We have mentioned three of the reasons: the capacity for humor, their realism, and the comfortable self-discipline they practice. But there is a fourth, and deeper, reason.

Zest, The Affirmation of Life

The zest is usually a sense of joy, or enJOYment, in living, which comes from a combination of self-commitment, now-living, and creativeness. The zest is a personal affirmation that old age is as much a time of creation, in its own way, as childhood, youth, or the middle years.

As usual, there is a lot of nonsense one can hear about the supposed "values" of old age and death, such as

- we can take comfort in the knowledge that when we depart this earth, we make room for the next generation;

- like the leaves which turn color in the fall, there is beauty in those who age gracefully;
- after one has worked long and hard during the middle years, one should enjoy the rewards of leisure, while the younger people provide for our caring.

I have sometimes wondered who makes up these little scenarios of half-truth and pious platitude. They do not remotely fit the stance of the zestful, seasoned oldsters' realistic view of themselves. Certainly, we shall all get around to the point of making room on the planet for the next generation. And quite soon enough too. But we are not all that keen about contributing to a sudden, big population shift!

The real point is that personal joy in older living is to be seen exactly where true zest is always experienced — at any age — in the most simple, direct consequence of *creative awareness.*

One spring day when Papa and Mama were still in their mid-eighties, I flew into southern Oregon during a business trip to visit them. After breakfast the next morning, we took a little walk around their backyard, where early flowers were beginning to bloom.

Each parent had begun to use a cane to walk safely outdoors. And, of course, I was using my customary two canes. We all laughed about now having ten "legs" among the three of us.

We stopped for a moment to look at a freshly leafed-out tree and Mama exclaimed, "Isn't it wonderful to be alive and to see all the growing things?"

Both Papa and I returned her smile as he said, "Yes, Myra," and I responded, "It sure is, Mama."

No one would associate that exchange with profound conversation. However, the incident occurred nearly 30 years ago, as of this writing. Yet, I recall it vividly today. Their zest at that moment intensely expressed the essence of what is meant by being alive.

Childhood and youth feel aliveness in great quantities. But the *quality* is no greater, if as great, as the aliveness known in older years![4] However, in order to experience that aliveness one must have established good emotional habit patterns during the young and middle years of life.

Compound Returns for Earlier Beginnings

If you find it necessary, or desirable, to make a new beginning after a crisis, there will usually be compensations quite soon in terms of greater confidence, inner balance, peace of mind, and enjoyment. Also, there will often be by-products in the form of unexpected material rewards. These, and other gains, will amply confirm that the decision and efforts in refocusing your life were wise.

Now, there is additional good news. The experiences of the older, zestful folk show that in their earlier years they got into the *habit* of generally following mature patterns of emotional health.

For instance, they tended to approach events with a sense of humor, objectivity, and the expectation of enjoyment. In tough spots they did not run away, even when frightened; they persisted. Increasingly, they tried to live one day at a time and to conduct themselves with moderation. As the chronology of age went by, there was little concern about attaching much significance to which birthday was ahead or behind.

Finally, they learned to place their emphasis upon what we call spiritual values and to assess other priorities accordingly.

CHAPTER 12
THE SPIRITUAL COMPONENT

The human experience includes four components — the physical, mental, emotional, and spiritual.

Ever since people began to use language, especially after the development of writing, humankind has been able to describe the nature of the physical and mental components. Understanding of the emotional area developed more slowly. It is only since the emergence of modern psychology that we have begun truly to describe the processes and potential of the emotional component. That happened mostly within this century.

In contrast, exploration of the spiritual component goes far back into human history. Indeed, ancient art and sculpture show that people were probing their spiritual experiences far back in what Thomas Mann called "the deep well of the past."

But, if our spiritual quest has been continuing so long, this raises an odd question: Why does such an important element of humanity remain an area of great confusion and disagreement? The cause of the disagreements is not lack of insight on the part of great spiritual leaders. Nor are we confused by the in-depth personal wholeness found by millions of searchers in the past.

Largely, the confusion of the creeds is probably rooted in the results of a strong human tendency.

We Organize Ourselves Into Groups

We are social beings. The hermits among us are vastly outnumbered by those who do things in social clusters — families, clans, neighborhoods, towns, and countries.

So, when someone with leadership ability has an in-depth spiritual experience, it is soon shared with a small group of followers. These individuals tend to band themselves into a permanent group, which seeks to share the insights they are enjoying with a wider number of people. Before long, a small religious organization is established. If this institution survives, it tends to grow. The new sect acquires the characteristics of a large religious movement: statements of belief, rituals, formal methods of teaching, and a method for continuing the succession of leadership.

(In a quick, capsule-like summary, we are describing now what happens over and over again in religious movements. To understand the distinctions between spirituality and religion, it is important to look at what happens among us historically.)

While all this takes place, experiences of spirituality continue to exist among *some* individuals and within *some* of the shared times of worship. But the component of spirituality tends to become identified more and more with the organization's forms and patterns of ritual by which the traditions are passed from generation to generation.

As different religions develop, each representing different religious-social streams in many parts of the world, sharp differences of opinion also occur about what is *the true path* to follow. When these issues collide with enough impact, or are combined with economic, territorial, or governmental issues, they have often led to armed conflict. Each side may claim in the middle of destroying one another to have the support of its supreme deity and to be the messenger of peace!

With succeeding generations, the accumulation of religious rite and dogma gets piled deeply into layers. An earnest seeker may need to do a lot of digging and excavation, so to speak, to discover the fragments of the cherished spiritual component.

However, if one has the patience to search, an odd and marvelous discovery is made. Within most of the major religions of the world and many of the minor groupings, experiences of the spiritual component can be found. Not only that, but instead of disagreement and confusion, one finds a high degree of wholeness, a similarity and a unity among all of the spiritual elements wherever they are found.

As simply now as possible, we shall try to define the nature of the spiritual component, as people experience it.

What Is It?

The essence of spirituality is the beginning which is ready to occur in each now.

That is what it is. You will immediately perceive that all through this book we have been discussing some of the methods by which people can exercise and grow in spirituality.

In attempting to describe the component, notice that the focus is upon words of active process, ". . . the *beginning* which is *ready* to *occur*. . . ." And then the accent upon, "now." This is the creativity, which is always in every true beginning, which is always waiting and prepared to occur, and which happens in a present moment.

So, what happens when we focus upon living in the now and we become open to the possibility of a new beginning? To the degree of our focusing and our openness, we then become partners in the activity of spirituality.

On the other hand, when we observe death and decay, or when we study the history of a great civilization that has fallen, it is easy to predict that hope is lost. This is true materialism.

The True Materialism

We usually think of materialism as a striving for things. However, that is only one of its many symptoms. The real materialism is based upon the assumption that life's most essential values are lost when physical bodies die or when civilizations fall. It is difficult for us to think otherwise, since so much of our effort and thought is expressed through material realities.

Some philosophers and spiritual-religious groups try to relieve themselves of the dual realities by claiming that the physical world is not true reality. They are trying to say that the material has no reality, since the ultimate is thought to lie in a spiritual area of universal mind or universal consciousness. The material components of our lives do have reality. We do not live with them well, if we try to divorce them mentally from the total realism of our experience in the universe. However, it is not our task, as we have earlier discussed, to ask this kind of "why question." It is our task to keep our values in some kind of rank order, so that we do not lose sight of, or fail to act upon, the priorities of the spiritual component.

As another illustration, when any individual has been immersed in his own troubles, is suffering from lack of confidence, fear, or too much emphasis upon the search for success, there is little perception of the now. Whenever we become immersed in any of the above whirlpools that take us out of life's mainstream, the only perception we have of the now is either

- a sense of desperation about time slipping away, or
- a show of bravado about our exaggerated ability to cope.

As a balance to our judgment, we need to remember always that even in the material realm this is a universe of counterweighted opposites. Decay, death, and even the fall of civilizations represent only one side of the material scale.

On the balance of the scale is creativity.

The Potential for Creativity

There are examples which remind us vividly of life and new beginnings.

Decay in the soil of the earth produces humus. The decay of dead and cast-off materials makes a rich compost in which seeds can sprout for the growth of new plants and trees.

On a grander scale, the element of carbon is an essential for life upon this planet. Yet the sources of that element are the cores of burned out, highly compressed dead suns.

Finally, and more personally, every individual human crisis brings with it the opportunity for some kind of new beginning. Were it not for the crises, we would often not give the intensity of concentration which opens us to creative events.

And this brings us to a practical question.

Where are we most apt to become aware of the spiritual component?

Spirituality comes with openness. The spiritual component is always potentially within us. But we are not always aware of it or moving in a direction where it can grow.

So, how do we open ourselves? We become seekers.

Seekers, Not Strivers

As suggested earlier, we need to have the right focus of direction. There is usually a need to surrender some of the egocentricity to the control of a Power greater than ourselves. Consciousness of spirituality and its growth occur as we stop trying to be God-manipulators and decide to be God-followers.

Immediately when the word "God" is mentioned, there will be a few individuals who will move into a mental or verbal pattern of God-denial. This is purely a mental/emotional exercise. From the spiritual component view, the denial maneuver has a different meaning from that of the avowed intention of the denier. In connection with spirituality, God-denial is merely a form of God-manipulation, a way of closing the door and saying, "Go away, God; get lost!"

On the other hand, most people play the role of God-manipulation simply by their focus of being ego-directed strivers, who attempt in one way or another to plan all aspects of their lives. Insofar as possible, they try to keep their inner selves closed in and isolated from the dangers of caring too deeply about other people or ultimate values. Of course, most of the time, while doing it, they are truly convinced this is the proper way to live. "This is the way one gets ahead."

Another avoidance pattern is that of misidentifying spirituality by using certain labels. This is usually one of the extensions of the confusion caused when we become so involved in organized religion that we miss the spiritual message within it. Spirituality is not a *something* that can be given a label, a name-image, or other recognition symbol. It is part of materialism to think in terms of name identification.

That can be appropriate when one is peddling soap or insurance or automobiles. One of the first tools an advertising firm uses is to devise an attractive company or product logo — a visual symbol that will aid potential customers to recall the name. That is good marketing.

In the spiritual area, however, it leads to evasion and the atrophy of growth. Fixation upon a name — a label — leads to evasion of the spiritual component.

This is the greatest blindness of all: The Nameless One has been with us, and we were not aware of it.

As observed in action, spirituality is a process. And a process is usually more difficult to understand because we cannot grasp it like a thing. We cannot grasp spirituality; it grasps us.

Idol worship is not confined to physical images. Idol worship occurs whenever we elevate any one thing to the point of making it worth our absolute loyalty, to the point where it interferes with the flow of love.

As we surrender our ego-striving, we become seekers. We begin to be open to the process of the spiritual.

One of the better examples of process, which helps us understand the meaning of creative beginning is the moment of birth.

The Birth of a Baby Person

The moment of birth becomes the focus of

1. intent,
2. personal functions,
3. life existence value,
4. sharing, and
5. joyful thankfulness.

All of these aspects of the moment have to do with human intention: certain functions which individuals carry out, both voluntary and through the biochemical processes; the values we attach to life; all the elements of sharing, including those of family; and the opportunities for joyful thankfulness in having a part of creativeness.

If one looks objectively at a newborn infant, the amazing thing is that persons become so excited about the event. Here is a small, red-faced individual, who demands a lot of attention, food, and patience. The infant will require several years' instruction to learn all the complicated things necessary to become an adult survivor. But no one looks at this individual as an object. The baby represents a miracle in the process of happening! In most instances, if there were any critic bold enough to question the validity and beauty of that miracle, he would be safer than someone attempting to molest the cubs of a mother grizzly bear.

So, let no one be scornful of the beauty and value of the spiritual component in our lives, which is also only observed in its processes.

Sustaining the Process

In maintaining the processes of physical, mental, and emotional health, each person has a role. We do not create the body, the brain cells, nor the electrochemical systems that enable us to feel emotions. But we always have definite decisions and actions to perform in seeing to it that we maintain our health in these areas.

We can also have a vital role in maintaining the functions and growth of the spiritual component within us. Although we did not create that element, its presence waits for us to open the door of our personal awareness. We can aid in sustaining the process by acting each day, as best we can, upon the realization that creativeness is THE proper human function.

In a Biblical creation story of the Old Testament this idea is expressed simply in the phrase, "Then God said, 'Let us create man in our own image. . . .' "[1] I assume this to mean, in part, that we are designed in such a way that the creative powers of love can flow through us in a variety of ways.

When a father or mother gives care to an infant and learns to give tough love at some of the later stages of youth development, the creative process is illustrated in two of its functions.

If someone labors with pleasure and dedication in an occupation that contributes something to society, the spiritual component is in operation. It does not matter what the name of the occupation may be, whether it be a digger of irrigation ditches or a painter of pictures in oil. Any task can be done with dignity and a sense of vocation, or it may be done unethically and merely for the material rewards. If the latter, the task will not involve the spiritual component.

That is each person's individual choice and responsibility.

Whenever we choose to perform our work with love and attention to doing it well, the work is not merely a job. It is a vocation — a giving of ourselves to others in the human family.

A spiritual component is operating then. This is what is meant, in part, by the ancient saying, "Work is prayer; prayer is work."

Another way we sustain spirituality is being willing to risk new beginnings. In my opinion, bold risk taking is not limited to the high adrenaline feats of mountaineers and other physical adventurers. How about the person who enters matrimony with the intent to remain with one mate for a lifetime? Or, any thoughtful married couple who decide to have another baby? What risks are involved when someone in midcareer decides to seek and begin a new skilled occupation? What about the middle-aged single woman, suddenly without eyesight, who decides to continue her career by making a new beginning with a guide dog and learning other skills, including braille?

These are risk-takers who quietly go about their purposes with great determination to let new beginnings happen through them. That takes more than belief or mere will-power. It requires true faith — a faith that the creative point of beginning is NOW. When people make such choices, many factors are in the equation, not the least of which is the spiritual component.

The author frequently meets with treatment center staffs who have used one of his earlier books as a group resource in recovery sessions. During such a recent discussion, one staff member asked, "What do you mean by maturity?"

Words such as *maturity, honesty,* or *serenity* cannot be understood in terms of persons, or role models, who may have arrived at certain levels of attainment. We can think of a physical life form, whether it be an apple or a human being, as having reached an approximate prime state of normal growth. There is a point at which a human child becomes man-sized or woman-sized. But in the areas of mental skill/wisdom and emotional maturity, growth may continue for almost the entire life span of a very old individual.

To an even greater degree, spirituality is difficult to encompass within boundaries and definitions. Early in this chapter we defined spirituality as "the beginning which is ready to occur in each now." That is as good a way as we know today to summarize how spirituality is perceived in action.

But are there analogies, or comparative pictures, which might help us to understand better the spiritual component?

Weaving a Tapestry

Sometimes human experience is compared to that of a person weaving a piece of fabric or a tapestry upon a loom. The spirituality, or the acts of love, may be said to be similar to the golden or brilliant yellow threads which go into the design. Like bright rays of the sun, they embellish and illuminate the more somber, less dramatic tones.

If we view life thus, however, the analogy soon breaks down, for the spiritual component is not merely one strand, nor one color. Love may be seen in the dark purple of pain, or in a dull color symbolizing the drudgery of a commitment to a monotonous daily task of serving a loved person.

There are no neat symbols for the different ways in which the creative process enters our lives, nor are there any limits to the endless variations among different individuals.

Instead of the spiritual component being one thread or a single strand in the fabric of each life, it is THE ESSENTIAL FUNCTION that gives the fullest meaning to all the other components.

The spiritual element is that strangest of all mysteries in life.

At one and the same time, it is:

the utterly simple, and the most
    awe-inspiring puzzle;
the point where each person becomes one with all,
    and each unique in specialness;
the beginning, and the end;

a meeting of choice with fateful destiny;
the unknowable bond of human consciousness
    with Ultimate Consciousness.

And here again, we come to that other mystery — the one which each person confronts whenever he concentrates long enough in relaxation and meditation upon the wholeness, the acceptance, the joyful meaning, or the simple beauty of life.

The mystery is perceived by each person in an individual way. But all who try to describe such experiences seem to include two similarities in their awareness.

There is a sense of a point nearby in the moment of NOW where a different dimension of space-time is present.

And, there is a sense of inner joy at the deepest level.

REFERENCES

Chapter One

1. Martha Miller, Rowayton, Conn., correspondence dated 2/28/85 and 3/12/85, concerning the original idea for this book and use of a quotation from her letter of 9/21/83.
2. *Alcoholics Anonymous,* Third Ed., A.A. World Services, New York, 1976, p. 60.
3. *Alcoholics Anonymous,* p. 59.
4. *The New English Bible,* Oxford University Press, New York, 1972, Ephesians 4:26.

Chapter Three

1. T. Canby Jones, "Thomas R. Kelly," *Living in the Light, Some Quaker Pioneers of the 20th Century,* ed. Leonard S. Kenworthy, Vol. I-In the U.S.A., Quaker Publications, Kennett Square, PA 1984.
2. The Reverend Dr. Culver H. Nelson, Minister, Church of the Beatitudes, Phoenix, Arizona.
3. Milton A. Maxwell, *The Alcoholics Anonymous Experience,* McGraw-Hill Book Co., New York, 1984.

Chapter Four

1. Robert Luccock, *Luccock Treasury,* Abingdon Press, Nashville-New York, 1963.

Chapter Five

1. *1973 Birth Defects: Atlas and Compendium,* Ed. David Bergsma, The Nat'l Foundation-March of Dimes, the William and Williams Co., Baltimore, 1973.
2. Jay Robert Nash, *Darkest Hours,* Nelson-Hall, Chicago, 1976.
3. Ibid.
4. William Fleming, *Arts and Ideas,* 6th edition, Holt, Rinehart, and Winston, New York, 1980.
5. Dietrick E. Thomsen, Senior Editor of Physical Sciences for *Science News,* Vol. 123, Feb. 19, 1983, p. 124. Reprinted with permission from SCIENCE NEWS, the weekly newsmagazine of science, copyright 1983 by Science Service, Inc.
6. Banesh Hoffman, *The Strange Story of the Quantum,* 2nd Ed., Dover Publications, New York, 1959, pp. 151, 152.
7. Culver H. Nelson, "Truth: Something You Do," sermon at Church of the Beatitudes (mimeographed), Phoenix, Arizona, Feb. 16, 1975.

Chapter Seven

1. Interviews with A. Hurford Crosman, Phoenix, Arizona, Jan. 1985.

Chapter Eight

1. Lewis F. Presnall, "Habakkuk After Hiroshima," *Advance,* Vol. 138, No. 9, Sept. 1946, pp. 25, 26.
2. Alan Jenkins, "Implications of the Atom Bomb," sermon at First Baptist Church and Central Congregational Church, Galesburg, Illinois, Aug. 19 and Oct. 7, 1945, (uncopyrighted, church printing).
3. Ernest Becker, *The Denial of Death,* The Free Press, New York, 1973, p. 156.
4. Soren Kierkegaard, *The Concept of Dread,* 1844, trans. Walter Lowrie, Princeton University Press, 1957, p. 41.
5. Lewis Thomas, *Late Night Thoughts on Listening to Mahler's Ninth Symphony,* The Viking Press, New York, 1980, pp. 164-168.

Chapter Nine

1. *The Brain,* Eds., David Lambert, Martyn Branwell, Gail Lawther, Perigee Books, G. P. Putnam's Sons, New York, 1982.
2. Ibid.

Chapter Ten

1. Joe Hudson, Gibson City, Illinois, verbal comment made at a workshop on retirement in Illinois, 1973. (Verified by personal correspondence July 1985.)
2. "The Wisdom of Sirach," 34: 9, 10, *The Apocrypha,* trans., Edgar J. Goodspeed, University of Chicago Press, Chicago 1938.

Chapter Eleven

1. Patricia A. Baur, Morris A. Okun, "Changes in Life Satisfactions In Late Life," *The Gerontologist,* Vol. 23, No. 3, April 1983, pp. 261-265.
2. Edward Demson, Phoenix, Arizona, conversations 1980-1982.
3. Robert J. Hannelly, "The View From Eighty-Two," article (mimeo.) Phoenix, Arizona, 1983.
4. Ibid.

Chapter Twelve

1. *The New English Bible,* Oxford University Press, New York, 1972, Genesis 1:26.

Other titles that will interest you...

Search for Serenity
by Lewis F. Presnall
"Some people meet life with zest; others seem to live in a state of chronic dissatisfaction. Those who are perpetually miserable, unhappy, and bored with life do not need to remain that way," writes the author. This book describes some of the practial ways to replace misery with serenity and is a helpful guide for anyone seeking peace of mind. Over a million copies in print. (152 pp.)
Order No. 6620

First Aid for Depression
by Lewis F. Presnall
Lewis F. Presnall has helped over a million people find peace of mind through his book *Search for Serenity*. Now, Presnall offers hope to those facing depression. Depression is a discomfort which can be endured through self-help action until professional services can be received. Based upon his own and others' experiences, Presnall describes first aid that can bring temporary relief for symptoms of depression. (11 pp.)
Order No. 5320

Each Day a New Beginning
The first daily meditation guide created by and for women involved in Twelve Step programs. Thousands of women and men from all walks of life have used this collection of thoughts and reflections to welcome each day with new hope, strength, and courage. (400 pp.)
Order No. 1076

For price and order information, please call one of our Customer Service Representatives.

Hazelden ®
Educational Materials

Pleasant Valley Road
Box 176
Center City, MN 55012-0176

(800) 328-9000
(Toll Free. U.S. Only)
(800) 257-0070
(Toll Free. MN Only)
(612) 257-4010
(AK and Outside U.S.)